·Cuisine Express·

· Cuisine Express ·

FOR PEOPLE WITH TASTE BUT NO TIME

Hilary Walden

WARD LOCK LIMITED · LONDON

Edited by Linda Sonntag
Designed by Niki fforde

Text set in Times New Roman
by Hourds Typographica, Stafford

Printed and bound in Italy by New Interlitho SpA

British Library Cataloguing in Publication Data

Walden, Hilary
Cuisine express : for people with taste
but no time.
1. Cookery
I. Title
641.5'55   TX652

ISBN 0-7063-6460-0

ACKNOWLEDGMENTS

Photography   David Burch
Chef   Jean-Louis Pollet

The publishers would like to thank
Frederick's Restaurant, Camden Passage,
London, for their assistance.

CONTENTS

INTRODUCTION

It is within the scope of any cook to prepare a snack, a single course or a complete meal that has a professional finish and shows flair, sophistication and originality in a very short time. It is possible to do this without recourse to convenience foods, an extensive collection of expensive modern cooking equipment or luxury ingredients such as caviar and foie gras. And you need not end up with a constant diet of stir-frys and salads. Poaching, steaming, grilling, baking, cooking 'en papillote' and even roasting and casseroling can all be used to produce an impressive variety of dishes in under an hour.

When time for cooking is short, quality and variety do not have to be sacrificed. The secret of success lies in using the correct cooking techniques and buying the most appropriate cuts of meat and fish, the right vegetables. You can dove-tail preparation and cooking and add a few skilful touches that will lend distinction very quickly and simply, such as the subtle use of herbs, spices and flavoured oils or vinegars.

The name for this style of cooking is 'Cuisine Express'. Meat, fish and vegetables are cooked quickly and lightly and sauces are prepared by the simple method of reduction rather than by the elaborate liaison of flour or eggs. Food is served in smaller, more digestible quantities, so it takes less time to prepare. Ingredients are extremely varied, so it is more interesting to eat.

The range of ingredients in supermarkets as well as high class delicatessens and ethnic shops seems to be increasing daily. Modern transportation and refrigeration bring fresh produce from far away places, so that root ginger, sweet potatoes, mangoes, pawpaw and passionfruit are now readily available. Exciting and successful attempts are being made by far-sighted horticulturists to cultivate species such as oyster mushrooms, that grew previously only in the wild; once popular varieties that mysteriously faded from favour, like scorzonera and celeriac and such exotica as mooli (white radish). So now you can find ingredients that used to be just words in cookery books on supermarket shelves. The revolution is such that shiitake mushrooms, which used to be a rare find in the dried state in specialist Oriental food shops, are now on sale, fresh, in the high street.

There has also been an enormous increase in the range of fish on sale both in fishmongers and at wet fish counters, and in line with popular recipes, butchers and meat counters now offer cuts such as mignons and noisettes. Game is even making an appearance in a few selected supermarkets with pheasant and venison, which is now farmed, taking the lead. To help inform the public, and to promote their products, supermarkets and chain stores as well as some enlightened producers and importers are producing helpful display material and leaflets alongside the 'new' foods.

The volume and variety of quality store-cupboard ingredients is also snowballing, as a walk around any good-sized food shopping area will reveal. Used judiciously, simple delicacies such as dried tomatoes packed in oil or black beans can be sensational, and I have included suggestions for these in the recipes. I would strongly advise buying any new ingredient that particularly catches your eye and experimenting with it to see how it can contribute to your cooking. You can always adapt 'standard' recipes to incorporate new foods and so add a variation on a theme.

In general, the quality of all our foods, both fresh and packaged, is improving. In the increasing number of good food shops it is already high and steadily getting better. This is very much to the advantage of 'Cuisine Express', as the basic quality of the ingredients, whether humble or exotic, is fundamental to the success of the cooking.

THE RECIPES All the recipes can be ready to eat in less than an hour. There are some that are prepared and cooked in a continuous flow, while others can be left to cook after the initial preparation, so allowing time to sit and have a drink, chat to guests or enjoy a preceding course.

Within each chapter the recipes have been arranged according to the time taken, the degree of complication or involvement and cost. They have been marked with appropriate symbols for further guidance. 'Guidance' is the operative word, as the time taken will vary according to individual speed and skill. What is straightforward to one is more difficult to another, and costs can vary with the time of year and the availability of ingredients.

If there is time during the cooking of a recipe for some basic preparation of ingredients, such as the chopping of shallots, this has been included in the method.

All recipes are for four people unless there is an indication to the contrary.

KEY

Denotes degree of cost

Denotes degree of complication

INGREDIENTS

*IMPORTANT BASIC
INGREDIENTS*

Stock

There is no substitute for home-made stock. No type of stock–whether game, fish, veal, brown veal or chicken–is difficult to make and none takes much time to prepare although, with the exception of fish stock which takes only about 20 minutes, they do take a while to cook. This should not cause any difficulties, as they can be left to simmer during the course of an evening or at the weekend, then kept, covered, in a jar or bowl in the refrigerator until required.

Fish stock should be re-boiled every other day; other stocks every 3 days to keep them 'sweet'.

Alternatively, if it is more convenient, the stock can be frozen in handy quantities, such as 175ml/6 fl oz, 225ml/8 fl oz and 300ml/$\frac{1}{2}$ pint.

Herbs

All herbs used in these recipes must be fresh. In summer, this should not create a problem as many, including parsley, chives, rosemary, tarragon, chervil, thyme, marjoram, summer savory, lovage, fennel, dill, sage, basil and sorrel, are easy to grow in even a small garden, providing it is not north-facing and completely screened from the sun. You can also grow herbs in tubs, pots or window boxes outside, and in mini-growbags or pots on the window sill indoors. Good greengrocers or supermarkets will keep you supplied if you can't grow your own.

Getting fresh herbs in the winter has been a problem for the cook, but now supplies are appearing all the year round in the best shops. Their flavour is often not as strong as in summer, so it will probably be necessary to use larger quantities. As tasting should be a matter of course during the preparation of all dishes there should be no fear of serving anything unintentionally bland–any lack will have been detected and remedied in the kitchen.

Wine

The 'body' as well as the quality of wine used in cooking is important. Inferior, thin and acidic properties are accentuated when a wine is concentrated by reduction, leaving a sauce that lacks distinction. Should a wine unexpectedly let you down and produce a disappointing sauce, then all is not lost. To rescue a white wine sauce, boil down 75–100ml/3–4 fl oz dry vermouth until it is reduced to about 1–2 × 15ml spoons/1–2 tablespoons, stir in some of the sauce, then stir this back into the main sauce. Or, for a more full-bodied white wine sauce, use fino sherry or sercial madeira. The remedy for red wine sauces is to treat them with port in a similar manner.

Examples of medium-bodied dry white wines that are suitable for cooking are Alsatian riesling, white Burgundies, Chablis (providing it is not of an inferior quality), modern-style (ie lighter) white Hermitage and Bulgarian chardonnay.

Examples of full-bodied dry white wines are Californian chardonnays, white Rhone and some of the bigger white Burgundies.

Suitable red wines are simple or petits châteaux wines from Bordeaux and the surrounding areas, such as Blaye, Bulgarian cabernet sauvignon, red Burgundies, Rhones and Californian cabernet sauvignon.

Butter
A good quality unsalted butter is recommended for all the relevant recipes in this book. Dice butter before melting it or adding it to sauces so that it will melt or be incorporated into the sauce more quickly.

STORE-CUPBOARD INGREDIENTS
Although the main ingredients of any meal should be fresh, the store cupboard can provide the inspiration and the little touches that add the stamp of originality and individuality. These extra touches should always be chosen with care and used with discretion. Chestnut purée is perfectly acceptable in its processed state, but other canned foods, such as artichoke hearts, are no substitute for the real thing.

Look out for products that are a little different but not 'gimmicky' and always search for quality. Some of the more expensive and unusual condiments on the delicatessen shelf can be made at home quite cheaply and with very little effort. For how to make flavoured oils, vinegars, mustards etc, see page 115 ff.

Some of the products used in the recipes are listed below. It is by no means an exhaustive or definitive list of store-cupboard ingredients; just advisory–a good starting-off point.

Oils
At the top of the list is good quality tasty, green virgin olive oil. You may also need a milder flavoured olive oil, flavourless oil for cooking, and walnut, hazelnut and flavoured oils (see page 126) for adding variety to salad dressings and in cooking.

Keep in a cool dark place for up to 4–6 weeks.

Vinegars
Choose from sherry, white wine, red wine, cider, tarragon and other herb and seed vinegars, raspberry and other fruit vinegars (see page 122).

Mustards
Including Dijon, Bordeaux, Meaux, wholegrain, tarragon and chive.

Spices
In the majority of cases these should be whole – cardamom pods, coriander seeds, vanilla pods, cloves, cinnamon sticks, nutmegs – but occasionally ground spice can also be useful. One particular example is ground mace. Add a little to a dressing–lemon juice, warmed cream or melted butter–toss in some prawns and see how the mace adds a new depth and dimension to their flavour.

Keep spices in airtight containers in a cool place away from direct light for no more than 3–4 months.

Dried wild mushrooms
Various types of dried wild mushrooms are available in packets from good grocers or specialist food shops. They are expensive for their weight, but are only used in small amounts. They must be soaked to reconstitute them before they can be used. Soaking times vary, so check with the instructions on the packet.

If fresh wild mushrooms are called for but not available, cultivated mushrooms can be 'beefed up' by the addition of just a few dried wild mushrooms.

Sun-dried tomatoes
These are available packed in oil from specialist Italian food shops and good grocers. They must be rinsed well, and are usually chopped before use. They impart a rich, deep tomato flavour.

Green or brown lentils
Unlike other pulses these do not need soaking, but can be cooked straight from the packet to provide the basis for all manner of interesting salads, or to serve as a vegetable.

Bulgur
This is cracked wheat that has been parboiled so that it is ready to use immediately, or after only about 5 minutes soaking in hot water, for salads, stuffings or as an accompaniment.

Gentlemen's relish
A traditional English savoury, intensely flavoured with anchovies that, when used sparingly, 'lifts' many a plain or bland dish and adds a slight piquancy to meat and poultry dishes as well as fish. (Anchovy used to be common as an all-purpose flavouring.)

Jars of fruits preserved in alcohol and syrup
Prunes in Armagnac, kumquats in Cointreau, peaches in whisky, cherries in kirsch etc, make a fitting finale to a good meal served either on their own, cold or warmed, or with a good ice cream, fromage blanc or Greek yoghurt.

FOODS TO STORE IN THE REFRIGERATOR

Fortunately, some of the foods that form the foundation of many dishes will keep for a few days in the refrigerator.

It is easy to forget that the quality of butters, creams and yoghurts can vary quite considerably from producer to producer, so do sample several. Rather than treating them as a 'regular' part of the routine shopping, count them as special purchases that are worth going out of your way to find.

Unsalted butter
All the recipes in the book requiring butter should be made with the unsalted variety.

Flavoured butters (see page 125)

Cream
Choose double, single or whipping cream according to individual preference. One type can often be substituted for another, provided account is taken of the difference in flavour, texture and consistency. If double is used instead of single, the dish will be richer and thicker, and the increase in the amount of fat will mask other flavours, including sweetness. You may want to take the according compensatory measures.

Crème fraîche
This is a French cream with a tangy, clean taste that gives a fresher flavour than ordinary British cream.

It is being sold by more and more supermarkets and grocers, but if it is not available a very passable alternative can be made at home by stirring some soured cream into twice the volume of whipping, or, for a richer product, double cream, then heating slowly to 90°C/194°F. Pour the cream into a jar and leave overnight in a warm place, about 75°C/167°F. Next day, stir the cream and place in the refrigerator. Crème fraîche tends to thicken on standing so it may be necessary to thin it with a little milk before using.

Cheese
It can be very useful to have a small selection of cheeses in the refrigerator to take the place of dessert, or to serve while the dessert is being prepared.

Many supermarkets and shops nowadays sell quite a number of different cheeses, but the pedigree and condition of the cheese are more important than variety. Patronize a counter where pride is taken in these particular aspects, where the assistant can offer sound advice about the cheeses and where you can buy the exact piece that you want. If cheese is to be kept for 2 or 3 days before being eaten, buy it slightly under-ripe. Make sure that it is well wrapped and kept in the coolest part of the refrigerator, then bring it to room temperature and loosen the wrapping at least 30 minutes, preferably longer, before it is served.

The most suitable cheeses for buying ahead are hard cheeses, blue cheeses and firmer goats cheeses.

Fromage blanc Soft, fresh French cheese that can be kept for 2–3 days. Provides an instant base for light soufflés and stuffings or marvellous desserts with fresh fruits or fruits bottled in alcohol.

Riccota cheese A soft, fresh Italian cheese that should be used immediately. It will not keep for more than a day or so. Use in the same way as fromage blanc.

Smoked meats and fish
The number of firms producing these is growing rapidly and the range of products is branching out from the traditional smoked salmon and trout to tuna, quail, duck, goose, chicken, poussins and all types of game.

The subtlety and pungency of the cure and the quality of the basic product vary enormously, so shopping around may be necessary. The majority of cured products are sold in vacuum packs. The wrapping should be removed and the product left at room temperature for up to 2 hours if possible to allow the flesh to 'breathe' and the flavour to develop.

Stocks (see page 116–17)

FOODS TO STORE IN THE FREEZER

A freezer or the freezing compartment of a refrigerator with a 3-star rating can be useful for keeping some 'back-up' foods.

Stocks (see page 116–17)

Filo pastry
With filo pastry it is possible to make delicious, crisp, melting pastries in a very short time – once the pastry has been made. Fortunately, filo pastry freezes well and can be used almost straight from the freezer. It does not require any rolling out and there is consequently no fear of shrinkage during cooking. Home-made filo (see page 118) does take a while and is quite laborious to prepare, but commercially made filo is perfectly acceptable.

Mussels

Mussels add an interesting character to many dishes but to prepare them fresh is quite time-consuming. Any slight loss of quality that might occur as a result of the freezing process is compensated for by the convenience of the frozen product and should not be detectable in the recipes in this book.

EQUiPMENT

The right equipment is as valuable an asset to the inexperienced cook as it is vital to the professional. It both saves time in preparation and improves the quality of the product.

With a knife that is sharp and the appropriate size, a carrot can be reduced to a pile of neat slices in a matter of moments. But use a knife that is blunt and unwieldy and either too small or too large, and the same carrot will be mutilated into untidy chunks while valuable time is lost sawing and scraping. It is undoubtedly much easier to become proficient at a task if the right equipment is used. The right size and weight of frying pan will produce meat that is brown and crisp on the surface. Crowd the same amount of meat into too small a pan and it will end up soft and pallid.

There is no need, though, to own a vast armoury of equipment. When buying anything for the kitchen, be selective, restrained and objective. Only buy what will be used often, or at least fairly frequently, and which performs the task that it is intended for efficiently and well. Don't buy anything you don't have room for.

Gadgets don't have to be shunned altogether. Some are very effective and can be a godsend. If stoned olives are your passion, an olive-stoner is a good buy; if fresh pasta is a particular favourite, a pasta-making machine is a worthwhile investment. But neither piece of equipment is worth bothering with if it will lie in the cupboard unused.

Not all so-called labour-saving equipment does, in fact, save labour, or time, or necessarily lives up to all the claims made by the manufacturers about its performance. This is especially true of multi-purpose equipment, such as food processors. Often one or two smaller, specialist pieces of equipment can be a more practical, rewarding and useful purchase. If your budget is limited, you would do better to buy an electric blender that can be used for making mousselines, puréeing and blending sauces (amongst other things) plus a selection of good knives that will neatly and efficiently cut all vegetables and herbs, than invest in a food processor. Of course, if space and money permit, all three would be even better still.

THE ESSENTIALS

There are certain pieces of equipment without which speedy, efficient cooking becomes very difficult or requires great skill.

The equipment listed here is sufficient for the preparation of all the recipes in this book and other similar recipes. It is not exhaustive, but forms a comprehensive basis on which to build, should you wish to.

Knives
The importance of good knives has already been mentioned. What makes a good knife is a blade that is sharp and firmly fixed into the handle with rivets; has a sharp point, if pointed; is well-balanced and comfortable to hold. A useful, basic selection would consist of:
a paring or vegetable knife with a short, sharp blade
a filleting knife with a flexible blade
2 or 3 cook's knives of different sizes
a small knife with a serrated blade
a bread knife
an all-purpose kitchen knife

Pots and pans

The size of saucepans and frying pans and what they are made of can make all the difference to the speed and quality of cooking. Choose good quality heavy pots and pans that will not dent or distort easily, have thick well-ground bases that will heat up evenly without 'hot spots', are well-balanced and have handles that are firmly attached and comfortable to hold. Lids should fit perfectly and have handles that are comfortable.

The size of frying pans is particularly important. With a 15, 17.5, 20 and 25cm/6, 7, 8 and 10 inch frying pan to choose from, you should always have the right size of pan for the quantity that is being cooked, from a snack for a single person to a main course for 4.

Non-stick coatings cut down on the time spent washing up after cooking, as well as the amount of fat needed during it.

A practical selection of saucepans would be three or four of varying sizes between 900ml/1½ pints and 2.4 litres/4 pints, with lids; a large, lidded saucepan for stocks, and a milk saucepan, or similar saucepan with non-stick coating and a good pouring lip.

Measuring equipment

You will need balance scales with two sets of weights, Imperial and metric; a set of measuring spoons; two measuring jugs, one for smaller amounts with gradations of 25ml/1 fl oz, and a larger one for about 1.2 litres/2 pints. Gradations for American cup measurements can be useful.

Miscellaneous

Other tools that are almost bound to be in your kitchen include the following:

wooden spatulas for stirring ingredients in saucepans and frying pans
a flexible palette knife or fish slice, for moving fish and meat without
    piercing the surface
tongs
a balloon whisk, for whisking butter into sauces
a steamer that will fit onto saucepans of various sizes
a chopping board
a perforated spoon, for removing solid food, herbs, whole spices etc.
    from a liquid
a colander and sieve
a multi-faceted grater, for fruit rinds and nutmeg
a knife sharpener and a magnetic rack to hold knifes
a juice extractor
a selection of bowls of different sizes
a potato peeler
a bottle opener
oven gloves
kitchen forks and spoons
kitchen scissors

USEFUL ADDITIONAL EQUIPMENT

For anyone who frequently prepares meals in a short time an electric blender will be more of a necessity than a useful extra. Other equipment that is useful but not essential includes:

a mandoline slicer, to produce thin, neatly sliced vegetables quickly
an electric steamer, to make steaming really trouble-free
a pot rest

sets of ramekin or similar individual dishes, of 1, 2 or 3 different sizes for cooking timbales, custards etc.

a roasting tin and a smaller baking tin, for placing the ramekins in to cook them

an electric ice cream maker, so that delicious home-made ice cream and sorbets (including some savoury ones) can be ready in next to no time

ACCESSORIES   Clingfilm, greaseproof paper and foil are useful for both storing and cooking food. Coffee making equipment is something that people often buy before they even have a kitchen.

CUISINE EXPRESS
COOKING

SAUCES

Thanks to modern cooking techniques it is now much easier to make light, smooth, glossy, delicious sauces, and create less washing-up than ever before.

With sauces made by reduction there is no time-consuming preliminary blending of flour or eggs with a liquid or vigilant, laborious stirring beset by worries that the sauce will be too thick or too thin or have the consistency of glue or scrambled egg. The time taken to make the sauce is governed by the amount of sauce to be made (the present trend for serving less sauce is a fortunate one when speed is of the essence); the volume of liquid to be reduced; the size of the pan being used, and the fierceness of the heat.

To speed up the operation use a large pan and a high heat so that the excess moisture will evaporate more quickly. If you are making a dish that calls for the sauce to be cooked in the pan with the meat or fish, you can partly reduce the sauce in a separate pan while the meat or fish is cooking. The reduced liquid can then be stirred into the cooking juices and the reduction completed.

Other tasks can usually be carried out during the early stages of a reduction, but a closer eye should be kept on the sauce as it approaches the required concentration, especially if the amount required is very small, such as a spoonful or two.

The instructions for the reduction of sauces can only be guidelines as strengths of stock and wine do vary. There is no substitute for tasting. The flavour can then be adjusted, if necessary, by further boiling or by dilution.

Should the flavour and consistency of a sauce be far too weak and thin, there is no need to pray for the best and resort to heavy seasoning, or throw the sauce away, providing there is some more stock or wine available. Simply boil some more in a separate pan until it is substantially reduced, then stir it into the sauce.

If you wish to serve more sauce than a recipe provides, increase both the 'before' and 'after' quantities, rather than not reducing the liquid to the degree recommended.

If you should add the butter too quickly or allow the sauce to boil once it has been made, the result will not be quite as smooth and shiny as a professional would wish, and the butter will separate out as the sauce cools. But all is not lost. Whisk the sauce and serve it quickly.

CHOOSING MEAT

Small, tender cuts of meat—fillets of beef, lamb, veal and pork, noisettes and medallions of lamb, veal and venison, mignons of venison and hare, escalopes of veal and pork, chicken and duck breasts – not only cook more quickly than larger less tender cuts, but can be cooked lightly and served 'pink'. Small pieces of meat such as cubes of pork or strips of beef will cook even faster, but there won't be any saving of time if you have to cut up the meat yourself, unless you can do it while something else is cooking.

Joints of meat need not be ruled out altogether as some can be cooked in a short time, such as fillet and loin of young lamb and veal and small whole birds like poussins, quails and squab (young pigeon).

Butchers have the right equipment and the experience to be able to bone meat quickly, effortlessly and efficiently, so ask the expert to prepare loin of pork, best end of lamb and noisettes. In fact, these cuts may be offered for sale already prepared (ask for the bones for making stock).

CHOOSING VEGETABLES

Choose small, young tender vegetables that will cook quickly and divide brassica such as cauliflower and broccoli into florets. The cooking time of artichokes can be reduced by cutting the head into quarters.

Steaming vegetables preserves their quality, flavour, colour, texture and nutritional value and is easier than boiling. More than one vegetable can be cooked over a single pan without the various flavours mingling into an overall 'vegetable' taste; timing is not as crucial; the cooked vegetables can be left 'in situ' to keep warm, if necessary, and there is no need to bother about straining them.

ORGANIZATION

A moment or two of reflection and forward thinking before you start to prepare a meal, or even a single dish, can save many minutes later. Take out everything you will need from the larder, cupboard and refrigerator beforehand. Use any spare time during cooking to prepare the ingredients to be used later on. Dove-tail all operations to speed up your overall timing.

LIGHT COURSES

Beetroot with orange dressing
Bulgur with peppers, herbs and cheese
Warm salad of mussels in black bean sauce
Prawn and beansprout salad
Steamed scallops with chive sauce
Fettucine with tuna, fennel and orange
Stilton and walnut salad with port dressing
Oyster and spinach toasts
Broccoli with warm orange yoghurt sauce
Prawns with garlic and ginger sauce
Smoked goose breast, pear and blackberry salad
Avocado pear with smoked oysters
Smoked duck breast with apple
Fresh sardines steamed with seaweed
Celeriac with hazelnuts
Chicken livers with paprika and yoghurt
Mushroom ragoût
Quails eggs in mushrooms
Fish cakes
Light rolled omelet with fish eggs
Grilled leeks with bacon and capers
Smoked salmon pikelets
Apple soup
Jerusalem artichoke salad
Prawns in crispy spinach blankets
Kedgeree
Jacketed eggs with tarragon sauce
Spinach dumplings
Goats cheese in vine leaves
Mozzarella cheese and tomato pastries
Baked jacket new potatoes with goats cheese pesto
Parsley 'tartlets' in lettuce leaves
Tomato and red pepper soup
Carrot soup
Mussels and tomatoes in croûtes
Leeks with smoked salmon and clams
Warm sorrel vichyssoise
Curried crab soufflés
Lettuce mousses with light smoked trout sauce
Green lentils with celery and pine kernels

BEETROOT WITH ORANGE DRESSING

 5 minutes

400g/14 oz freshly boiled
   beetroot, diced

FOR THE DRESSING

2 × 15ml spoons/
   2 tablespoons walnut oil
2 × 15ml spoons/
   2 tablespoons olive oil
3 × 15ml spoons/
   3 tablespoons orange juice
10ml spoon/2 teaspoons
   grated orange rind
2.5ml spoon/$\frac{1}{2}$ teaspoon
   wholegrain mustard
salt and freshly ground black
   pepper
15ml spoon/1 tablespoon
   crushed coriander seeds,
   lightly toasted

FOR THE GARNISH

watercress

For the dressing, whisk together the oils, orange juice and rind, mustard, salt and pepper. Add the coriander seeds.

Toss the beetroot in the dressing and serve with a garnish of watercress.

BULGUR WITH PEPPERS, HERBS AND CHEESE

 10 minutes

100g/4 oz bulgur
75g/3 oz Feta cheese
$\frac{1}{2}$ red pepper
$\frac{1}{2}$ green pepper
6 spring onions
3 × 15ml spoons/
   3 tablespoons finely
   chopped parsley
6 × 15ml spoons/
   6 tablespoons finely
   chopped basil
freshly ground black pepper

Pour 350ml/12 fl oz boiling water over the bulgur and leave for about 5 minutes, until the water has been absorbed.

Meanwhile, chop the cheese, red and green peppers and the spring onions. Stir the cheese, vegetables, herbs and black pepper into the bulgur.

Serve warm.

WARM SALAD OF MUSSELS IN BLACK BEAN SAUCE

 10 minutes

15ml spoon/1 tablespoon oil,
  preferably sesame
5ml spoon/1 teaspoon finely
  chopped garlic
1½ × 15ml spoons/
  1½ tablespoons coarsely
  chopped canned black beans
15ml spoon/1 tablespoon
  finely chopped spring onions
5ml spoon/1 teaspoon soy
  sauce
15ml spoon/1 tablespoon
  Marsala
75ml/3 fl oz fish stock or
  water
¼ red pepper
curly endive or chicory
2.5ml spoon/½ tsp cornflour
24 large shelled mussels, fresh
  or frozen

Heat a non-stick frying pan, add the oil, garlic, black beans and spring onions and stir together. Heat for a minute, then stir in the soy sauce, Marsala and stock or water. Bring to the boil and simmer for about 5 minutes.

Meanwhile, blanch and dice the red pepper and shred the endive or chicory.

Blend the cornflour with 15ml/1 tablespoon water, then stir into the sauce and cook, stirring, until the sauce thickens. Remove from the heat and carefully stir in the mussels to warm them through.

Place the curly endive or chicory to one side of 4 small plates. Spoon the mussels next to it and sprinkle with red pepper.

PRAWN AND BEANSPROUT SALAD

 10 minutes

4 × 15ml spoons/
  4 tablespoons thick lemony
  mayonnaise (see page 119)
4 × 5ml spoons/4 teaspoons
  Ricard or Pernod
1 spring onion, very finely
  chopped
225g/8 oz shelled prawns
75g/3 oz beansprouts
75g/3 oz cucumber, diced
crisp lettuce leaves, shredded
2.5ml spoon/½ teaspoon finely
  chopped tarragon

Blend the mayonnaise and Ricard or Pernod together, then add the spring onion.

Lightly toss together the prawns, beansprouts and cucumber.

Lightly fork the mayonnaise through the prawn mixture.

Divide the lettuce leaves between 4 cold plates and spoon the prawn mixture into the centre.

Sprinkle the tarragon over.

WARM SALAD OF MUSSELS
IN BLACK BEAN SAUCE

21

STEAMED SCALLOPS WITH CHIVE SAUCE

 10 minutes

16 scallops
300ml/½ pint fish stock
200g/7 oz fromage blanc
15ml/1 tablespoon finely
chopped chives
scant 1.25ml spoon/¼ teaspoon
Meaux mustard
salt and freshly ground white
pepper

FOR THE GARNISH

finely grated lemon rind

Remove the scallops from their shells, separate the corals from the bodies and cut into halves horizontally. Place on a sheet of greaseproof paper in a single layer and steam for 2 minutes.

Meanwhile, boil the stock in a frying pan until reduced to 50ml/2 fl oz. Stir in the fromage blanc, chives, mustard, salt and pepper and warm through, but do not allow to boil.

Spoon onto 4 warmed plates and arrange the scallops on top.

Sprinkle a little finely grated lemon rind over the scallop bodies for garnish.

FETTUCINE WITH TUNA, FENNEL AND ORANGE

 10 minutes

25g/1 oz unsalted butter,
diced
15ml spoon/1 tablespoon olive
oil
1 small bulb of fennel, thinly
sliced
350g/12 oz fresh fettucine
salt and freshly ground black
pepper
100g/4 oz smoked tuna or
lambs tongues, sliced
75ml/3 fl oz cream
1 orange, peeled, divided into
segments, pith and skin
removed

FOR THE GARNISH

finely chopped parsley

Heat the butter and oil, add the fennel and cook, stirring occasionally, for 2-3 minutes.

Meanwhile, cook the fettucine in boiling salted water for 1 minute. Cut the tuna or tongue into strips.

Drain the fettucine very well and return to the rinsed pan. Place over a low heat, then toss in the fennel and cream, then the tuna or tongue, orange, salt and pepper. Heat through gently for a minute or two.

Serve sprinkled with plenty of chopped parsley.

Note: Dried fettucine can be used if fresh is not available. Cook it before cooking the fennel for the length of time given on the packet.

STEAMED SCALLOPS
WITH CHIVE SAUCE

23

STILTON AND WALNUT SALAD WITH PORT DRESSING

 10 minutes

15g/½ oz unsalted butter
75g/3 oz walnuts, coarsely
    chopped
1 head of oak leaf lettuce or
    small head radicchio
1 head of lambs lettuce
1 small head of curly endive
100g/4 oz Stilton, roughly
    crumbled

FOR THE DRESSING

5ml spoon/1 teaspoon Dijon
    mustard
2 × 15ml spoons/
    2 tablespoons mild olive oil
5ml spoon/1 teaspoon
    hazelnut or walnut oil
5ml spoon/1 teaspoon red
    wine vinegar
5ml spoon/1 teaspoon lemon
    juice
15ml spoon/1 tablespoon
    tawny port
salt and cayenne pepper

First make the dressing by blending all the ingredients together in a liquidizer or whisking by hand.

Heat the butter, add the nuts and cook, stirring occasionally, for 2 minutes, then remove the nuts with a perforated spoon and drain on absorbent paper.

Toss the salad leaves with about one third of the dressing, then arrange on 4 plates. Toss the nuts in another third of the dressing and scatter over the salad. Scatter the Silton over the salad and sprinkle the remaining dressing over the cheese.

Serve immediately.

OYSTER AND SPINACH TOASTS

 10–15 minutes

4 slices French bread
unsalted butter, for spreading
Gentleman's relish
squeeze of lemon juice
5ml spoon/1 teaspoon olive oil
10ml spoon/2 teaspoons finely
    chopped shallot
50g/2 oz spinach, shredded
5ml spoon/1 teaspoon sherry
    vinegar
4 oysters

Spread the slices of bread with butter, then a very little Gentleman's relish. Sprinkle with a little lemon juice, then place in a hot oven, 220°C/425°F/Gas 7 for 5–8 minutes until crisp.

Meanwhile, heat the oil, add the shallots and cook for about 3 minutes over a moderate heat. Add the spinach and cook until it has softened, but still retains its shape, and there is no surplus liquid. Sprinkle the vinegar over.

Form a nest of spinach on each toast and place an oyster in the centre.

BROCCOLI WITH WARM ORANGE YOGHURT SAUCE

 15 minutes

400g/14 oz broccoli florets
salt, freshly ground black
    pepper
90ml/6 tablespoons fino sherry
approx 1½ × 15ml spoons/
    1½ tablespoons sesame
    seeds, optional
3 × 15ml spoons/
    3 tablespoons concentrated
    orange juice, frozen or from
    a carton
175ml/6 fl oz thick yoghurt

Steam the broccoli over salted water for 8–10 minutes until just tender.

Meanwhile, boil the sherry until reduced to 2 × 15ml spoons/ 2 tablespoons.

Lightly toast the sesame seeds in a non-stick pan, if using.

Stir the orange juice and yoghurt into the reduced sherry and whisk with a wire whisk until warmed. Season with salt and black pepper.

Arrange the broccoli on 4 warmed plates and spoon the sauce over. Sprinkle with sesame seeds, if using.

PRAWNS WITH GARLIC AND GINGER SAUCE

 15 minutes

1½ × 15ml spoons/
    1½ tablespoons sesame oil
450g/1 lb peeled prawns
1 garlic clove, crushed
1½ × 5ml spoons/
    1½ teaspoons finely chopped
    fresh ginger
1 shallot, finely chopped
100ml/4 fl oz fish stock
5ml spoon/1 teaspoon soy
    sauce
75ml/3 fl oz fino sherry
75ml/3 fl oz double cream
25g/1 oz mangetout peas
25g/1 oz young carrots
25g/1 oz white part of leek
salt, freshly ground black
    pepper
lemon juice

Heat the oil in a large frying pan over a moderately high heat and cook the prawns, stirring, for 2 minutes. Remove the prawns with a perforated spoon and drain on absorbent paper.

Stir the garlic, ginger and shallot into the pan and cook for 10 seconds.

Stir in the stock, soy sauce and sherry and boil until reduced by half. Stir in the cream and reduce by one third.

Meanwhile cut the mangetout peas, carrot and leek into fine strips, then blanch for 1 minute in boiling salted water. Refresh and drain well.

Return the prawns to the sauce and heat through gently. Season with salt, pepper and lemon juice.

Divide between 4 warmed plates and scatter the vegetables over to serve.

SMOKED GOOSE BREAST, PEAR AND BLACKBERRY SALAD

 10 minutes

2 ripe pears, about 100g/4 oz each
1½ × 15ml spoons/1½ tablespoons lime juice
10ml spoon/2 teaspoons grated lime rind
10ml spoon/2 teaspoons olive oil
salt, freshly ground white pepper
4 slices smoked goose breast or 50g/2 oz Westphalian ham
1 small head of chicory
1 head of radicchio or 2 heads chicory
50g/2 oz blackberries

Peel and core the pears. Thinly slice one and sprinkle with a few drops of lime juice. Purée the other with the remaining lime juice, the lime rind, oil, salt and pepper.

Cut the smoked goose breast or ham into strips.

Arrange the salad leaves and slices of pear on 4 small plates, then add the goose breast and blackberries and spoon a little of the pear dressing around.

AVOCADO PEAR WITH SMOKED OYSTERS

 10 minutes

8 smoked oysters
1 just hard-boiled egg yolk
few drops Tabasco sauce
15ml spoon/1 tablespoon lemon juice
3 × 15ml spoons/ 3 tablespoons olive oil
salt, freshly ground black pepper
2 ripe avocado pears

FOR THE GARNISH

sprigs of flat-leaved parsley

Drain the oil from the oysters.

Mash the egg yolk, then gradually work in the Tabasco sauce, lemon juice and oil to make a thick, smooth sauce. Season with salt and pepper, taking care not to add too much salt.

Cut the avocado pears in halves lengthways and remove the stones. Spoon a little of the sauce into the cavities left by the stones, place 2 oysters in each cavity and spoon the remaining sauce over them.

Garnish with sprigs of flat-leaved parsley.

SMOKED GOOSE BREAST,
PEAR AND BLACKBERRY SALAD

SMOKED DUCK BREAST WITH APPLE

 10 minutes

5ml spoon/1 teaspoon finely
   crushed coriander seeds,
   toasted
4 × 15ml spoons/
   4 tablespoons apple juice
5ml spoon/1 teaspoon extra
   virgin olive oil
salt, freshly ground black
   pepper
a pinch of sugar
1 large Cox's Orange Pippin
   apple
lemon juice
fresh coriander
8 slices of smoked duck
   breast, fat removed
curly endive
approx 3 × 15ml spoons/
   3 tablespoons finely
   chopped red pepper

Mix the coriander seeds, apple juice and oil together and season with salt, pepper and sugar.

Core and slice the apple and sprinkle with lemon juice.

Place a frew fresh coriander leaves on 4 cold plates. Place the smoked duck breast on top. Arrange curly endive, slices of apple and the red pepper beside the duck.

Stir the dressing and spoon over the duck.

FRESH SARDINES STEAMED WITH SEAWEED

 10 minutes + 5 minutes soaking

approx 20g/¾ oz wakame
   (dried seaweed), soaked for
   5 minutes
8 fresh sardines, cleaned and
   scaled
freshly ground black pepper
4 × 15ml spoons/
   4 tablespooons lemon juice

Squeeze the water from the wakame, then place half in a layer in a steaming basket. Lay the sardines on top, season with black pepper then cover with the remaining wakame.

Steam for 4–5 minutes until tender.

Warm the lemon juice gently in a small saucepan.

Arrange the wakame on 4 warmed plates, add the sardines and sprinkle them with lemon juice.

FRESH SARDINES
STEAMED WITH SEAWEED

CELERIAC WITH HAZELNUTS

 15 minutes

450g/1 lb celeriac
40g/1½ oz unsalted butter
3 × 15m spoons/
    3 tablespoons lemon juice
40g/1½ oz hazelnuts, lightly
    toasted, chopped
salt, freshly ground black
    pepper

FOR THE DRESSING

4 × 15ml spoons/
    4 tablespoons soured cream
1½ × 5ml spoons/
    1½ teaspoons clear honey
10ml spoon/2 teaspoons
    Meaux mustard
approx 5ml spoon/1 teaspoon
    lemon juice
salt, freshly ground pepper

First make the dressing by blending together the soured cream, honey, mustard, lemon juice, salt and pepper.

Peel the celeriac and cut into small dice. Heat the butter over a moderate heat, add the celeriac and cook, stirring the pieces around with a wooden spoon, for about 2 minutes.

Stir in the lemon juice and let it bubble for a minute or so.

Stir in the nuts and a little salt and pepper. Remove the celeriac from the heat, stir in the dressing and serve immediately.

CHICKEN LIVERS WITH PAPRIKA AND YOGHURT

 15 minutes

25g/1 oz unsalted butter
450g/1 lb chicken livers, sliced
1 small shallot, finely chopped
4 × 5ml spoons/4 teaspoons
    paprika
150ml/5 fl oz medium-bodied
    dry white wine, optional
225ml/8 fl oz chicken stock
300ml/½ pint set plain yoghurt
5ml spoon/1 teaspoon tomato
    purée
salt

Heat the butter in a frying pan, add the livers and shallot and cook over a moderate heat for 2 minutes, stirring gently and frequently to ensure the livers cook evenly.

Transfer the livers to a warmed plate with a perforated spoon.

Stir the paprika into the pan and cook for 1-2 minutes, stirring. (If the pan is too dry add a little of the stock.) Stir in the wine, if using, and boil until reduced to about 15ml/1 tablespoon. Stir in the stock and boil hard until reduced to 50ml/2 fl oz. Stir in the yoghurt and boil, stirring occasionally, until reduced to 100ml/4 fl oz.

Stir in the tomato purée and salt, boil briefly, lower the heat, add the livers and heat briefly.

Spoon onto 4 warmed plates.

MUSHROOM RAGOÛT

 15 minutes

25g/1 oz unsalted butter,
   diced
3 × 15ml spoons/
   3 tablespoons finely
   chopped shallots
400g/14 oz oyster mushrooms,
   cut into 1.5cm/½ inch slices
50ml/2 fl oz medium-bodied
   dry white wine
100ml/4 fl oz sercial madeira
50ml/2 fl oz double cream
2.5ml spoon/½ teaspoon
   chopped caraway seeds or
   1½ × 15ml spoons/1½
   tablespoons finely chopped
   parsley
salt, freshly ground black
   pepper
lemon juice

Heat the butter in a frying pan, add the shallots and cook over a moderate heat, stirring occasionally, for 2–3 minutes until slightly softened but not coloured.

Stir in the mushrooms and cook for 2–3 minutes.

Add the wine and madeira and cook until reduced by half.

Stir in the cream and caraway seeds, if used, and cook for 4–5 minutes or until thickened slightly.

Season with salt, pepper and lemon juice.

Serve sprinkled with the parsley if caraway seeds have not been used.

QUAILS EGGS IN MUSHROOMS

Serves 2 or 4

 15 minutes

50g/2 oz unsalted butter,
   diced
2 shallots, finely chopped
60ml/4 tablespoons
   medium-bodied red wine
4 large flat mushrooms
5ml spoon/1 teaspoon finely
   chopped parsley
pinch of finely chopped
   rosemary
salt, freshly ground black
   pepper
white wine vinegar
4 quails eggs

FOR THE GARNISH

small sprigs of parsley

Heat 15g/½ oz butter in a small saucepan, add the shallots and half of the wine, cover and cook over a fairly low heat for 3–4 minutes until softened and the wine has evaporated.

Meanwhile, heat 25g/1 oz butter in a frying pan, add the mushrooms and cook over a moderate heat for 3–4 minutes, turning them over half-way through.

Meanwhile, add the remaining wine and the parsley and rosemary to the shallots and swirl in the remaining butter. Season with salt and pepper and keep warm over a low heat.

Bring a shallow pan of water just to simmering point. Add a little white wine vinegar, then carefully break in the quails eggs. Poach gently for 2 minutes.

Place the mushrooms on absorbent kitchen paper then on 4 small warmed plates. Spoon the shallot mixture onto the mushrooms. Carefully remove the eggs from the poaching liquid with a perforated spoon and place on top of the shallots. Garnish with small springs of parsley.

LIGHT ROLLED OMELET
WITH FISH EGGS

FISH CAKES

 15 minutes

400g/14 oz skinned salmon
    fillet
sea salt, freshly ground white
    pepper
pinch of cayenne pepper
5ml spoon/1 teaspoon lemon
    juice

FOR THE DRESSING

15ml spoon/1 tablespoon
    lemon juice
3 × 15ml spoons/
    3 tablespoons olive oil
5ml spoon/1 teaspoon soy
    sauce
2 spring onions
salmon eggs or caviar,
    optional

FOR THE GARNISH

coriander leaves and fine
    shreds of spring onion

With a very sharp flexible-bladed knife, cut the salmon into very small dice.

Carefully transfer the dice to a cold bowl, sprinkle with sea salt, white pepper, cayenne pepper and lemon juice and toss lightly. Cover and chill for 30 minutes.

For the dressing, whisk together the lemon juice, oil and soy sauce. Finely chop the spring onions and mix into the dressing.

Drain the liquid from the salmon. Form the salmon into cakes. Place on cold plates. If using salmon eggs or caviar, form a small indentation in the top of each cake and place a few fish eggs in the wells.

Whisk the dressing again, check the seasoning and spoon around the cakes.

Garnish with coriander leaves and shreds of spring onion.

LIGHT ROLLED OMELET WITH FISH EGGS

  10 minutes + 6 minutes cooking

4 eggs, separated
3 × 15ml spoons/
    3 tablespoons finely
    chopped chives
salt, freshly ground black
    pepper
150ml/5 fl oz soured cream or
    thick Greek yoghurt
50g/2 oz salmon eggs, caviar
    or lump fish roe

FOR THE GARNISH

small lettuce leaves, eg oak
    leaf or radicchio

Whisk the egg whites until stiff. Break up the egg yolks, then gently fold into the whites with the chives, salt and pepper until just evenly mixed.

Lightly spread the mixture into a Swiss roll tin, approx 30 × 18.5cm/10 × 7½ inches, lined with well buttered greaseproof paper. Bake for about 6 minutes at 180°C/350°F/Gas 4 until set and pale golden.

Immediately spread the soured cream or yoghurt over the omelet. Quickly sprinkle with the salmon eggs, caviar or lump fish roe and roll up with the aid of the greaseproof paper like a Swiss roll.

Cut into 12 slices and place, cut side up, on 4 small warmed plates. Garnish the plates with small lettuce leaves.

GRILLED LEEKS
WITH BACON AND CAPERS

 15–20 minutes

6–8 long, slim leeks
salt, freshly ground black
* pepper*
75g/3 oz lightly salted lean
* bacon, finely chopped*
15ml spoon/1 tablespoon
* finely chopped shallot*
50ml/2 fl oz dry vermouth
175ml/6 fl oz double cream
15ml spoon/1 tablespoon
* chopped, drained capers*
2.5ml/½ teaspoon Dijon
* mustard*
melted butter
10ml spoon/2 teaspoons finely
* chopped flat-leaved parsley*

Trim the leeks of their roots and all but the most tender green parts. Cook in simmering salted water until just tender, about 4 minutes.

Meanwhile, cook the bacon in a frying pan, preferably non-stick, over a moderately high heat, stirring occasionally, until crisp. Pour off excess fat, add the shallot and cook for 1 minute over a moderate heat, stirring occasionally.

Add the vermouth and boil rapidly until almost evaporated.

When the leeks are cooked, drain them well and dry with absorbent paper.

Stir the cream into the frying pan, add the capers, pepper and mustard, and boil for 2–3 minutes until slightly thickened.

Meanwhile season the leeks with pepper, then brush with melted butter, place about 10cm/4 inches away from a hot grill, and cook for 4–5 minutes, brushing with melted butter and turning occasionally until lightly browned and crisp on the outside and creamy soft in the centre.

Reduce the heat beneath the thickened sauce, adjust the seasoning and keep warm over a low heat.

Serve the leeks whole with the sauce spooned over or beside them, or cut the leeks into thick slices, arrange, cut side up, on 4 small warmed plates, and spoon the sauce into the centre.

Sprinkle the parsley over the sauce.

SMOKED SALMON PIKELETS

 15–20 minutes

50g/2 oz self-raising flour
5ml spoon/1 teaspoon baking
* powder*
pinch of mustard powder
freshly ground black pepper
1 egg, beaten
90ml/6 tablespoons milk
15ml spoon/1 tablespoon
* melted unsalted butter*
40g/1½ oz smoked salmon,
* finely shredded*
soured cream, lemon wedges
* and salmon eggs, caviar or*
* lump fish roe, to serve*

FOR THE GARNISH

sprigs of parsley

Sieve the flour, baking powder and mustard powder together and season with black pepper. Form a well in the centre, add the egg, milk and butter and mix with a fork to a smooth batter. Stir in the smoked salmon.

Smear a large non-stick frying pan or electric griddle plate with butter. Heat over a moderately high heat, then add a tablespoonful of the salmon mixture. Spread the mixture out slightly and cook for 1½–2 minutes until bubbles rise to the surface and the underside is a light golden brown. Turn over and cook for about another minute until the underside is browned.

Transfer to a warm plate and keep warm in a folded tea towel while cooking the remaining mixture.

Serve while still as warm as possible with soured cream, lemon wedges and salmon eggs, caviar or lump fish roe. Garnish with sprigs of parsley.

APPLE SOUP

 20 minutes

350g/12 oz Bramley's
  Seedlings, cored and
  quartered
lemon juice
350g/12 oz Cox's Orange
  Pippins, cored and
  quartered
175ml/6 fl oz medium-bodied
  fruity dry white wine
2 cinnamon sticks
3 cloves
40ml/1½ fl oz calvados
175ml/6 fl oz chicken stock
100ml/4 fl oz crème fraîche or
  50ml/2 fl oz each double
  and soured cream
salt, freshly ground white
  pepper

Reserve a Bramley's quarter and sprinkle with lemon juice. Bring the remaining apples, wine, cinnamon and cloves to the boil, cover and simmer for about 10 minutes, until the apples are tender.

Remove the cinnamon and cloves, then purée the apples with the calvados, stock and crème fraîche or soured and double cream.

Cut the reserved apple into fine strips. Reheat the soup, stirring gently, but do not allow it to boil. Season with salt and pepper.

Serve garnished with the apple strips.

JERUSALEM ARTICHOKE SALAD

 20 minutes

550g/1¼ lb smooth young
  Jerusalem artichokes
salt
finely grated rind of 1 lemon
4 × 15ml spoons/
  4 tablespoons mayonnaise
  (see page 119), made with
  lemon juice and preferably
  half and half walnut and
  olive oil
15ml spoon/1 tablespoon
  sunflower seeds

Cook the artichokes in simmering salted water for about 12 minutes until just tender.

Meanwhile, whisk 2 × 15ml/2 tablespoons warm water and the lemon rind into the mayonnaise.

Drain the Jerusalem artichokes, hold them in a tea-towel and remove their skins, then cut into 2cm/¾ inch pieces.

Fold in the dressing and sprinkle the sunflower seeds over. Serve warm.

P R A W N S   I N   C R I S P Y
S P I N A C H   B L A N K E T S

 20 minutes

12 raw Mediterranean or
   Dublin Bay prawns
6 × 15ml spoons/
   6 tablespoons lime juice
sea salt, a pinch of cayenne
   pepper
approx 12 young spinach
   leaves
3 × 15ml spoons/
   3 tablespoons dry vermouth
3 × 15ml spoons/
   3 tablespoons lemon juice
100g/4 oz cold unsalted
   butter, diced
freshly ground white pepper
freshly grated nutmeg

Carefully remove the legs and the shells from the bodies of the prawns, but leave the heads and tails in place. Remove the dark vein that runs along their backs. Toss in lime juice seasoned with sea salt and a pinch of cayenne pepper and leave to marinate, if possible, for anything up to an hour.

Trim the stalks from the spinach leaves.

Remove the prawns from the juice and dry on absorbent kitchen paper. Wrap each prawn tightly in 1 or 2 spinach leaves, leaving the heads and tails exposed. Secure the leaves with wooden cocktail sticks.

Carefully lower the prawns into hot deep oil, 180°C/350°F, and cook for 6–8 minutes until crisp.

Meanwhile, boil the vermouth and lemon juice until reduced to 15ml/1 tablespoon.

Reduce the heat to very low and gradually whisk in the butter, making sure each piece is fully incorporated before adding the next. Season with salt, pepper and nutmeg.

Drain the prawns on absorbent kitchen paper, remove the cocktail sticks and serve immediately accompanied by the sauce.

K E D G E R E E

  20 minutes

100g/4 oz long-grain rice
salt, freshly ground black
   pepper
25g/1 oz butter
2 shallots, chopped
approx 5ml spoon/1 teaspoon
   curry powder, to taste
225g/8 oz courgettes, thinly
   sliced
225g/8 oz skinned and boned
   cooked salmon, flaked
15ml spoon/1 tablespoon
   lemon juice
4 × 15ml spoons/
   4 tablespoons soured cream

FOR THE GARNISH

sprigs of parsley

Cook the rice in boiling salted water for about 12 minutes or until just tender.

Meanwhile, heat half of the butter, add the shallots, stir in the curry powder and cook, stirring frequently, for 2–3 minutes.

Stir in the courgettes and cook, turning frequently but gently, for about 3 minutes, so they remain crisp.

Drain the rice very well and return to the rinsed pan.

Over a very low heat fork in the salmon, heat for a minute or so, then carefully add the courgette mixture. Season with lemon juice and black pepper, then briefly fork through the soured cream.

Serve garnished with sprigs of parsley.

PRAWNS IN
CRISPY SPINACH BLANKETS

JACKETED EGGS WITH TARRAGON SAUCE

 20 minutes

4 spinach leaves, stalks
   removed
butter
4 eggs
salt, freshly ground black
   pepper

FOR THE SAUCE

175g/6 oz unsalted butter,
   diced
15ml spoon/1 tablespoon
   tarragon vinegar
2 × 15ml spoons/
   2 tablespoons lemon juice
3 egg yolks
2 × 15ml spoons/
   2 tablespoons finely
   chopped tarragon

Blanch the spinach leaves in boiling water for 1½ minutes. Refresh under cold running water and drain very well.

Butter 4 individual ovenproof dishes well, then line each one with a spinach leaf–part of each leaf should extend over the sides of each dish.

Break an egg into each dish, season lightly with salt and pepper, then carefully fold the overlapping leaf over. Place the dishes in a roasting tin and surround with boiling water. Cover the dishes with foil and put in a moderate oven, 180°C/350°F/Gas 4 for 6–8 minutes, until the eggs are just set.

Meanwhile, in separate saucepans, heat the butter until it has melted and the vinegar and lemon juice until simmering.

Briefly blend the egg yolks in a blender or food processor then, with the motor running, pour in the vinegar and lemon juice in a slow, steady stream.

When thoroughly incorporated, pour in the butter in the same way to make a thick, airy sauce. Add salt, pepper and tarragon.

Remove the dishes from the heat and leave for a minute or so before unmoulding.

Serve the eggs accompanied by the warm sauce.

SPINACH DUMPLINGS

 20 minutes

900g/2 lb spinach, shredded
75g/3 oz butter
200g/7 oz Ricotta cheese
1 egg
approx 75g/3 oz seasoned
   plain flour
25g/1 oz fresh Parmesan,
   finely grated

Cook the spinach with about 2 × 15ml spoons/2 tablespoons water until it has 'fallen' and excess moisture has evaporated. Drain very well, squeezing out as much water as possible.

Melt half the butter, add the spinach and cook, stirring occasionally, for 2 minutes. Remove from the heat and beat in the cheese, egg and 3 × 15ml spoons/3 tablespoons flour.

Form the mixture into small, cork-shaped dumplings and roll them in the remaining flour.

Bring a large pan of salted water to simmering point and slip the dumplings in. Cook gently for 5–8 minutes until they rise to the surface. Remove with a slotted spoon and keep warm.

Melt the remaining butter, trickle over the dumplings and sprinkle the cheese over.

GOATS CHEESE IN VINE LEAVES

 10 minutes + 10 minutes cooking

8 pieces of sun-dried tomato in olive oil

100–125g/4–5 oz goats cheese

75ml/3 fl oz olive oil

8 fresh vine leaves (if fresh vine leaves are not available, use canned or bottled ones–rinse them well and soak in hot water for 20 minutes)

4–8 slices French bread

Gently pound the tomatoes until very thin.

Cut the cheese into slices with a wetted sharp knife.

Dip each piece of cheese in olive oil.

Dry the vine leaves very well and trim off the stems.

Sandwich each piece of cheese between 2 pieces of tomato and wrap in 2 leaves. Brush the packages with oil and grill for about 5 minutes each side.

Meanwhile, rub the bread with olive oil, then bake in a moderate oven, 180°C/350°F/Gas 4 for about 7 minutes until crisp and golden.

Place a goats cheese package on a slice of toasted bread. Serve with extra toasted bread to scoop out the melted cheese.

MOZZARELLA AND TOMATO PASTRIES

Makes about 8

 15 minutes + 7 minutes cooking

2 sheets filo pastry

approx 40g/1½ oz melted unsalted butter, blended with 5ml/1 teaspoon Dijon mustard

approx 65g/2½ oz Mozzarella cheese

beaten egg

2 small–medium tomatoes, sliced

salt, freshly ground black pepper

poppy seeds

FOR THE GARNISH

sprigs of parsley

Brush the filo with the butter and mustard. Place the pastry sheets one on top of the other and cut in half.

Cut circles that are slightly larger than the diameter of the tomatoes from one half, then cut circles slightly larger than that from the other half.

Cut the cheese into circles a little smaller than the pastry circles.

Brush the tops of the smaller pastry circles with egg and place a piece of cheese on each. Place a slice of tomato on top. Season with salt and pepper. Cover with the remaining pastry circles, pressing the edges together firmly to seal. Brush with beaten egg and sprinkle with poppy seeds.

Place on a greased baking sheet and bake in a fairly hot oven, 200°C/400°F/Gas 6 for 6–7 minutes until light golden.

Serve hot, garnished with parsley.

PARSLEY TARTLETS
IN LETTUCE LEAVES

BAKED JACKET NEW POTATOES WITH GOATS CHEESE PESTO

 10 minutes + 10–15 minutes cooking

400g/14 oz small new potatoes
salt, freshly ground black
    pepper
sprig of thyme
75g/3 oz goats cheese, rinds
    removed
25g/1 oz soft cheese
25g/1 oz chopped basil
10ml spoon/2 teaspoons lemon
    juice
15ml spoon/1 tablespoon
    walnut oil
15ml spoon/1 tablespoon olive
    oil
40–50g/1½–2 oz unsalted
    butter

Simmer the potatoes in salted water to which the sprig of thyme has been added for about 6–8 minutes, until almost tender.

Meanwhile, purée the cheese, with the basil, lemon juice and oils in a blender. Season with salt and pepper.

Melt the butter in a baking tin.

Drain the potatoes well. Put into the baking tin and turn to coat in the butter. Sprinkle liberally with pepper, then place in a hot oven, 220°C/425°F/Gas 7, for about 10–15 minutes, until just tender.

Serve the potatoes piping hot to be cut through and topped with sauce.

PARSLEY TARTLETS IN LETTUCE LEAVES

 10 minutes + 15 minutes cooking

4 medium–large lettuce leaves
1½ eggs
2 egg yolks
65ml/2½ fl oz double cream
50g/2 oz soft cheese
12 × 15ml spoons/
    12 tablespoons finely
    chopped parsley
salt, freshly ground black
    pepper
5ml spoon/1 teaspoon olive oil
flesh of approx 550g/1¼ lb
    large tomatoes, chopped
small sprig of oregano
approx 2.5ml spoon/
    ¼ teaspoon tomato purée

FOR THE GARNISH

flat-leaved parsley

Remove the thick stalks from the lettuce leaves, then blanch the leaves for 30 seconds. Drain, refresh under cold running water, then dry well on absorbent kitchen paper.

Line 4 buttered ovenproof dishes with the leaves. Place in a roasting tin.

Lightly beat the eggs, egg yolks, cream and cheese together. Add the parsley and season with salt and pepper.

Divide the mixture between the lettuce leaves, surround the dishes with boiling water, cover with greasproof paper and cook in a moderate oven 180°C/350°F/Gas 4 for 12–15 minutes until just set.

Meanwhile, heat the oil, add the tomatoes and oregano and cook for 10 minutes.

Remove the oregano and stir in salt, pepper and tomato purée to enrich and slightly thicken the sauce.

Leave the tartlets to stand before easing them out of the dishes so the lettuce leaves remain underneath. Place on warmed plates with a little of the sauce. Garnish the sauce with a leaf of flat-leaved parsley.

TOMATO AND RED PEPPER SOUP

 25–30 minutes

4 × 15ml spoons/
   4 tablespoons olive oil
700g/1½ lb large ripe
   tomatoes, chopped
1 red pepper, chopped
2 shallots, finely chopped
1 bay leaf, broken
approx 600ml/1 pint chicken
   stock
15ml spoon/1 tablespoon
   finely chopped basil
salt, freshly ground black
   pepper

FOR THE TOASTS

4 anchovy fillets, split in half
milk
4 slices crusty French bread
olive oil, for brushing
freshly ground black pepper
4 slices Bel Paese

Heat the oil, add the tomatoes, red pepper, shallots and bay leaf. Stir, then simmer for about 10 minutes, stirring occasionally.

Stir in the stock and simmer for a further 10 minutes.

For the toasts, soak the anchovy fillets in milk for about 10 minutes.

Brush the bread with olive oil and season with freshly ground black pepper. Place a slice of cheese on top, put on a baking tray and place in a fairly hot oven, 190°C/375°F/Gas 5, for about 10–15 minutes until crisp and golden.

Purée the soup, pass through a sieve, return to the rinsed pan, add the basil, season with salt and pepper and reheat. Adjust the consistency, if necessary, adding more stock if too thick, boiling down if too thin.

Drain the anchovy fillets and place in a cross on the top of each toast. Serve with the soup.

CARROT SOUP

 15 minutes + 25 minutes cooking

15ml spoon/1 tablespoon oil
40g/1½ oz smoked bacon
   trimmings, chopped
2 shallots
450g/1 lb carrots (not large
   ones)
75ml/3 fl oz dry vermouth
approx 750ml/1¼ pints
   chicken stock
4 × 15ml spoons/
   4 tablespoons double cream
salt, freshly ground white
   pepper
10ml spoons/2 teaspoons
   finely chopped lovage or
   chervil

Heat the oil, add the bacon and cook over a moderately low heat for about 3 minutes until the fat begins to run, stirring occasionally.

Meanwhile, chop the shallots. Stir the shallots into the bacon and cook for about 2 minutes, stirring occasionally.

Meanwhile, finely chop the carrots, then add to the shallots and bacon, increase the heat slightly and cook for 3 minutes, stirring occasionally.

Stir in the vermouth and boil to reduce by half, then add the stock. Bring to the boil.

Reduce the heat, cover and simmer gently for 25 minutes.

Meanwhile, mix the cream with the salt, pepper and lovage or chervil.

Purée the soup in a blender, return to the rinsed pen and reheat.

Season and adjust the concentration and consistency, if necessary, by adding more stock or boiling down.

Divide the soup between 4 warmed bowls and add a spoonful of the cream to each one.

MUSSELS AND TOMATOES IN CROÛTES

 30 minutes

100g/4 oz unsalted butter,
  diced
15ml spoon/1 tablespoon each
  finely chopped rosemary,
  thyme, parsley and basil
½ a sandwich loaf, preferably
  2 or 3 days old
2 small shallots
16 mussels, shelled
75ml/3 fl oz dry vermouth
15g/½ oz unsalted butter
flesh of 4 tomatoes, diced
5ml spoon/1 teaspoon finely
  chopped fennel
salt, freshly ground black
  pepper

Gently heat the butter in a small saucepan. Add the herbs as it begins to melt, then leave to melt completely and heat it until it begins to foam at the sides. Cover and remove from the heat.

Cut the bread into 4 and remove the crusts to leave pieces about 4cm/1½ inches square by 6.5cm/2½ inches deep. With a small sharp knife and a teaspoon scoop out the centre from each piece of bread, leaving a border of about 5mm/¼ inch all the way round.

Brush all the surfaces of the bread croûtes with the melted butter, place on a baking tray and bake in a moderately hot oven, 200°C/400°F/Gas 6, for 15 minutes until crisp and golden.

Meanwhile, chop the shallots, then cook with the mussels and vermouth for 3 minutes. Swirl in the butter then add the tomatoes, fennel, salt and pepper.

Divide the mussels and tomatoes between the baked croûtes and serve immediately.

LEEKS WITH SMOKED SALMON AND CLAMS

 30–35 minutes

2–3 large leeks
salt, freshly ground black
  pepper
8 small slices of smoked
  salmon
lemon juice
8 large clams, out of their
  shells
8 × 5ml spoons/8 teaspoons
  lightly seasoned fromage
  blanc
100ml/4 fl oz fish stock
75ml/3 fl oz medium-boiled
  dry white wine
40ml/1½ fl oz dry vermouth
175g/6 oz fromage blanc
150ml/5 fl oz thick plain
  yoghurt
approx 1½ × 15ml spoons/
  1½ tablespoons chopped
  fennel

FOR THE GARNISH

strips of red pepper

Make a lengthways slit through the outer layers of the leek leaves. Remove 8 large leaves and blanch these in boiling salted water for 1½–2 minutes, then drain and refresh under cold running water. Drain, then dry well between sheets of absorbent paper.

Lay them out flat and line with a piece of smoked salmon. Sprinkle with a squeeze of lemon juice. Place a clam near the base of each leaf, then top with 5ml/1 teaspoon lightly seasoned fromage blanc.

Roll up each leaf against the grain to enclose the clam. Place, seam side down, in a buttered, flameproof dish, pour the stock, wine and vermouth around, season with salt and pepper and bring just to simmering point.

Cover with greaseproof paper and cook gently for 3–4 minutes. Carefully transfer the packages, still under the greaseproof paper, to a warmed plate and boil the juices rapidly until reduced to 15ml/1 tablespoon.

Remove from the heat, stir in the fromage blanc and yoghurt, then place over a low heat and whisk until warm and frothy.

Add the fennel, adjust the seasoning, then spoon over 4 warmed plates. Place 2 packages on each plate. Garnish each package with strips of red pepper.

WARM SORREL VICHYSSOISE

Serves 6

 10 minutes + 25–30 minutes cooking

50g/2 oz butter
2 shallots, finely chopped
2 slim leeks, chopped
300g/10 oz potatoes
1 litre/1¾ pints chicken stock
225g/8 oz sorrel
100ml/4 fl oz double cream
salt, freshly ground white
    pepper

Heat the butter, add the shallots and leeks and cook over a moderately low heat for 3 minutes, stirring occasionally.

Peel and chop the potatoes and stir into the leeks. Cook for 3 minutes, stirring occasionally. Do not allow any of the vegetables to brown.

Stir in the stock, bring to the boil, then lower the heat and simmer for 25–30 minutes until the potatoes are very tender.

Meanwhile, shred the sorrel finely.

Purée the soup in a blender with most of the cream and most of the sorrel. Warm the soup through gently – do not allow it to boil. Season with salt and pepper and add a little more stock if the soup is too thick.

Pour into 4 warmed soup bowls, swirl in the remaining cream and sprinkle the remaining sorrel over.

CURRIED CRAB SOUFFLÉS

  10–15 minutes + 12–15 minutes cooking

25g/1 oz unsalted butter
2 × 15ml spoons/
    2 tablespoons finely
    chopped shallots
10ml spoon/2 teaspoons curry
    powder, to taste
350g/12 oz crabmeat, flaked
2 egg yolks
175g/6 oz Ricotta cheese or
    sieved cottage cheese
salt, freshly ground black
    pepper
squeeze of lemon juice
4 egg whites

Heat the butter, add the shallots and cook for about 3 minutes, stirring occasionally, until softened but not coloured.

Stir in the curry powder and cook for about 2 minutes.

Remove the pan from the heat and stir in the crab and egg yolks, then the cheese. Season to taste with salt, pepper and lemon juice.

Whisk the egg whites until stiff but not dry, then gently fold into the crab mixture.

Divide the mixture between 4 buttered ovenproof dishes, approx 175ml/6 fl oz each, and bake in a moderate oven, 180°C/375°F/Gas 4, for 12–15 minutes, until risen and light golden.

LETTUCE MOUSSES WITH LIGHT SMOKED TROUT SAUCE

 10 minutes + 15–20 minutes cooking

2 heads of round lettuce,
    quartered
225ml/8 fl oz double cream
3 eggs
celery salt, freshly ground
    white pepper
lemon juice

FOR THE SAUCE

50g/2 oz smoked trout fillet
4 × 15ml spoons/
    4 tablespoons cottage
    cheese
4 × 15ml spoons/
    4 tablespoons thick plain
    yoghurt
2.5ml spoon/½ teaspoon lemon
    juice
scant 2.5ml spoon/½ teaspoon
    horseradish cream

TO DECORATE

sprigs of chervil or fennel

Cook the lettuces in boiling water for 1½–2 minutes, refresh under cold running water, then press down firmly on them to remove excess moisture. Chop them.

Lightly whisk the cream and eggs together. Add the lettuce, celery salt, pepper and lemon juice to taste.

Divide between 4 buttered individual ovenproof dishes. Place the dishes in a baking tin and surround them with boiling water. Cover the tops of the dishes with greaseproof paper and cook in a moderate oven, 180°C/350°F/Gas 4, for about 15–20 minutes, until just set in the centre.

Meanwhile, purée the ingredients for the sauce.

Remove the dishes from the heat and leave to stand for a minute or two before unmoulding onto warmed plates.

Spoon the sauce beside the moulds and garnish with sprigs of chervil or fennel.

GREEN LENTILS WITH CELERY AND PINE KERNELS

  5 minutes + 40 minutes cooking

100g/4 oz green lentils
2 sticks celery, sliced
1 small lime
40g/1½ oz pine kernels or
    flaked almonds

FOR THE DRESSING

4 × 15ml spoons/
    4 tablespoons olive oil
2 × 15 ml spoons/
    2 tablespoons sherry
    vinegar
10ml spoon/2 teaspoons
    Meaux mustard
salt, freshly ground black
    pepper

Boil the lentils for 10 minutes, then cover and simmer for 30 minutes.

Meanwhile, shake all the ingredients for the dressing together.

Slice the celery. Remove the peel and pith from the lime and chop the flesh. Discard any pips.

Drain the lentils very well then stir in the celery, lime and nuts. Shake the dressing once more then stir into the lentils. Serve warm.

FISH AND SHELLFISH

Warm salmon salad
Prawn and crab patties
Red mullet with warm mint sauce
Salmon and turbot parcels
Monkfish and broad bean ragoût
Fillets of sole with cucumber and mint
Turbot with aromatic herbs and tomatoes
Salmon chowder
Trout with light herb filling
Trout filled with watercress and almonds
Sole with scallops and coral sauce
Seafood lasagne
Salmon with red vermouth sauce
Poached turbot with coriander and cream sauce
Seafood brochettes with coconut sauce
Salmon with lemon balm and vanilla sauce
Fettucine with a duo of salmon
Sole with cucumber mousse

WARM SALMON SALAD

 15 minutes

15g/1½ oz unsalted butter
350g/12 oz skinned salmon
   fillet, cut into 2cm/¾ inch
   wide strips
15g/½ oz fresh ginger, peeled
   and finely chopped
3 × 15ml spoons/
   3 tablespoons very finely
   chopped shallot
50ml/2 fl oz rice wine vinegar
   or fino sherry
juice of 1 lime
15ml spoon/1 tablespoon soy
   sauce
salt and freshly ground black
   pepper
10ml spoon/2 teaspoons
   walnut oil
100ml/4 fl oz olive oil
2 × 15ml spoons/
   2 tablespoons chopped
   coriander leaves or parsley

TO SERVE
curly endive
approx 2 × 15ml spoons/
   2 tablespoons chopped pine
   nuts

Heat the butter in a non-stick frying pan, add the salmon and cook for about 2 minutes, turning the strips so they cook evenly. Transfer with tongs to absorbent kitchen paper.

Mix the ginger, shallot, rice wine vinegar or sherry, lime juice, soy sauce, salt and pepper together, then whisk in the oils, or mix briefly in a blender.

Mix the coriander or parsley into the dressing.

Divide the endive and salmon between 4 plates, then sprinkle some of the dressing over each one and scatter pine nuts over. Serve the remaining dressing separately.

PRAWN AND CRAB PATTIES

 15 minutes

90g/3½ oz Dublin Bay prawn
   flesh, fresh or frozen,
   chopped
salt, freshly ground black
   pepper
1 egg
50ml/2 fl oz double cream
350g/12 oz crabmeat, fresh or
   frozen
1 ripe tomato, skinned, seeded
   and finely chopped
½ bunch of chives, chopped
25ml/1 fl oz olive oil

Purée the Dublin Bay prawn flesh in a blender or food processor.

Add the salt and pepper, then gradually add the egg and cream, mixing well after each addition. Mix with the crab, the tomato flesh and the chives.

Season and form into 12 small oval cakes about 2cm/¾ inch thick.

Place the cakes on a baking sheet, brush with olive oil and bake in a hot oven, 200°C/400°F/Gas 6 for 5–7 minutes.

When the cakes are lightly browned, remove from the oven but leave on the baking sheet for about 5 minutes before carefully removing with a fish slice.

RED MULLET
WITH WARM MINT SAUCE

48

RED MULLET WITH WARM MINT SAUCE

15–20 minutes

175ml/6 fl oz fish stock
75ml/3 fl oz medium-bodied
  dry white wine
25ml/1 fl oz dry vermouth
2 × 15ml spoons/
  2 tablespoons finely
  chopped shallot
3 × 15ml spoons/
  3 tablespoons finely chopped
  mint
long strip of lemon peel
8 red mullet fillets
salt, freshly ground black
  pepper
3 × 15ml spoons/
  3 tablespoons extra virgin
  olive oil
15ml spoon/1 tablespoon
  white wine vinegar

Heat the stock, wine, vermouth, shallot, 2 × 15ml spoons/2 tablespoons mint and the lemon peel to simmering point in a shallow pan that is just large enough to hold the fish in a singler layer.

Add the fish, cover with greaseproof paper, reduce the heat so the liquid barely moves, and poach for about 3–4 minutes.

Carefully lift out the fish using a fish slice, season with salt and pepper, cover and keep warm.

Boil the cooking liquid until only about 25ml/1 fl oz remains. Stir in the oil and the vinegar and bring to the boil. Pass through a sieve. Add the remaining mint.

Place the fillets on warmed plates and spoon the sauce over.

SALMON AND TURBOT PARCELS

20 minutes

2 red peppers, seeded and
  chopped
8 large chard leaves, stalks
  removed
15ml spoon/1 tablespoon
  lemon juice
225g/8 oz skinned salmon
  fillet, cut into 4 pieces
freshly ground black pepper
4 sprigs of dill
450g/1 lb skinned turbot fillet,
  cut into 4 pieces

Cook the peppers gently in 150ml/5 fl oz water in a covered saucepan for about 20 minutes, until soft.

Meanwhile, cook the chard leaves in boiling salted water for 5 minutes.

Sprinkle lemon juice on the salmon and season with a little black pepper. Put a sprig of dill on each piece.

Drain the chard, refresh under cold running water and dry on absorbent paper.

Sandwich each piece of salmon between two pieces of turbot. Season with pepper, then wrap each sandwich securely in 2 chard leaves. Tie with string, like a parcel.

Place the parcels in the top part of a steamer, cover then cook over boiling water for 5 minutes.

Purée the peppers, then reheat in a clean pan. Season to taste.

Remove the string from the fish parcels.

Spoon sauce over 4 warmed plates. Cut about three-quarters of the way through each parcel and place, partially opened out, on the sauce.

MONKFISH AND BROAD BEAN RAGOÛT

 20 minutes

25g/1 oz unsalted butter
2 × 15ml spoons/
    2 tablespoons finely
    chopped shallots
700g/1½ lb boned monkfish
    tail, skinned and cut into
    approx 3cm/1¼ inch cubes
350g/12 oz shelled young
    broad beans, or thawed
    frozen broad beans
1 sprig of summer savory
175ml/6 fl oz medium-bodied
    dry white wine
175ml/6 fl oz crème fraîche
salt, freshly ground white
    pepper
approx 4 × 5ml spoons/
    4 teaspoons finely chopped
    savory

Heat the butter, add the shallots and cook over a moderatly low heat for about 3 minutes.

Add the fish and cook over a moderate heat, stirring occasionally, for 2 minutes.

Meanwhile, blanch the broad beans (if using fresh beans) in boiling salted water for 1 minute. Drain well. Add the beans to the fish with the savory and wine, cover and cook gently for about 3 minutes until the beans and fish are just tender.

Transfer the fish and beans to a warmed plate with a perforated spoon.

Boil the cooking juices with the savory until reduced to a light syrupy consistency. Stir in the crème fraîche and boil to reduce to a smooth sauce. Adjust the seasoning, remove the savory and spoon the sauce over the fish and beans. Sprinkle over a little more summer savory.

FILLETS OF SOLE WITH CUCUMBER AND MINT

  25 minutes

1 medium-sized cucumber,
    peeled, cut in half
    lengthways, seeds removed
4 fillets of sole, about
    175g/6 oz each, skinned
100ml/4 fl oz fish stock
100ml/4 fl oz medium-bodied
    dry white wine
15ml spoon/1 tablespoon
    finely chopped shallot
175ml/6 fl oz crème fraîche
13 medium mint leaves
sea salt, freshly ground white
    pepper
2 × 15ml spoons/
    2 tablespoons unsalted
    butter, diced

Cut the cucumber in half lengthways again, then cut each piece into 3 strips. Cut these into 5cm/2 inch lengths.

Fold the fillets in half, skinned side innermost.

Put the stock and wine into a frying pan that the fish will just fit and make a bed with the shallots in the bottom. Place the fillets on the shallots and heat the liquid to just below simmering point. Cover the fish with buttered greaseproof paper and poach gently for about 4 minutes until the flesh becomes opaque.

Carefully transfer the fish to a warmed plate with a fish slice and cover loosely.

Bring the poaching liquid to the boil and continue to boil until the liquid is reduced to about 65ml/2½ fl oz.

Add the cucumber, stir the crème fraîche into the liquid and boil again until it starts to thicken.

Pour any liquid that has seeped from the fish into the sauce. Boil again if necessary.

Chop 5 of the mint leaves and add to the sauce with the salt and pepper.

Reduce the heat to very low and swirl in the butter.

Place the fillets on plates, spoon the sauce around and garnish with the remaining mint leaves.

MONKFISH AND
BROAD BEAN RAGOÛT

TURBOT WITH AROMATIC HERBS AND TOMATOES

 15 minutes + 12 minutes cooking

*3 × 15ml spoons/
3 tablespoons finely
chopped shallots
4 fillets of turbot, about
175g/6 oz each, skinned
15ml spoon/1 tablespoon
lemon juice
flesh of 6 tomatoes, chopped
15ml spoon/1 tablespoon
finely chopped rosemary
2 × 15ml spoons/
2 tablespoons chopped
parsley
15ml spoon/1 tablespoon
chopped thyme
1 bay leaf, crumbled
salt, freshly ground white
pepper
15ml spoon/1 tablespoon olive
oil
150ml/5 fl oz full-bodied dry
white wine
150ml/5 fl oz fish stock
40g/1½ oz unsalted butter,
diced*

Sprinkle the shallots over the base of a buttered shallow dish that the fish will fit in a single layer.

Lay the turbot on top, sprinkle with lemon juice and cover with the tomatoes.

Mix the herbs with the salt and pepper. Sprinkle over the tomatoes and sprinkle the oil on top.

Bring the wine and stock to the boil. Pour around the fish, cover and cook in a moderately hot oven, 190°C/375°F/Gas 5 for about 10 minutes.

Transfer the fish to a warmed serving plate and keep warm. Bring the cooking juices to the boil and reduce to about 175ml/6 fl oz. Then, over a very low heat, gradually swirl in the butter.

Spoon the sauce onto 4 warmed plates and place the fish on top. Garnish the fish with sprigs of flat-leaved parsley, if liked.

SALMON CHOWDER

 25 minutes

*12 small new potatoes, skins
left on
2 shallots, finely chopped
1 bay leaf, broken
300ml/½ pint milk
450g/1 lb skinned salmon fillet
225ml/8 fl oz fish stock
6 parsley stalks
50ml/2 fl oz double cream
15g/½ oz unsalted butter
salt, freshly ground white
pepper*

FOR THE GARNISH

chopped parsley

Put the potatoes in a small saucepan that they will just fit in a single layer. Add the shallots, bay leaf and milk, cover and simmer for 12–15 minutes until the potatoes are just tender.

Meanwhile, cut the salmon into approx 3cm/1¼ inch pieces, then poach in the stock with the parsley stalks for 2–3 minutes.

Remove the potatoes, bay leaf and as many of the pieces of shallot that can easily be scooped up from the milk with a perforated spoon and keep warm. Boil the milk until reduced to about 75ml/3 fl oz, stirring occasionally to make sure that it does not catch on the bottom of the pan.

Meanwhile, lift out the salmon with a perforated spoon and keep warm with the potatoes. Boil the stock until reduced to 50ml/2 fl oz.

Stir the milk and cream into the stock, remove the parsley stalks and boil briefly. Reduce the heat and swirl in the butter. Season with salt and pepper and add the fish and potatoes. Turn to coat in the sauce, then serve garnished with parsley.

SALMON CHOWDER

TROUT WITH LIGHT HERB FILLING

 10 minutes + 20 minutes cooking

150g/5 oz sole or whiting
  fillets, skinned and chopped
1 small egg white
3 × 15ml spoons/
  3 tablespoons single cream
2 × 15ml spoons/
  2 tablespoons finely
  chopped parsley
2 × 15ml spoons/
  2 tablespoons finely
  chopped chives
10ml spoon/2 teaspoons finely
  grated lemon rind
salt, freshly ground black
  pepper
25g/1 oz unsalted butter
25g/1 oz small spinach leaves
4 trout
50ml/2 fl oz fish stock
3 × 15ml spoons/
  3 tablespoons dry vermouth

Purée the sole or whiting in a blender or food processor, then add the egg white, cream, herbs, lemon rind, salt and pepper and mix until very smooth.

Spread the butter over a shallow dish that is large enough to hold the fish and lay the spinach leaves on top.

Season the trout inside and out and divide the sole filling between them. Place on the spinach and pour the stock and vermouth over. Cover the dish with foil and cook in a moderate oven at 180°C/350°F/Gas 4 for about 20 minutes.

Transfer the fish to a warmed serving plate. Boil the cooking juices to thicken them slightly, then spoon, with the spinach, next to each fish.

TROUT FILLED WITH WATERCRESS AND ALMONDS

 15–20 minutes + 15 minutes cooking

175g/6 oz watercress
100g/4 oz cottage cheese
3 × 15ml spoons/
  3 tablespoons ground
  almonds
salt, freshly ground black
  pepper
4 trout, boned if possible
lemon juice
120ml/8 tablespoons medium-
  bodied dry white wine
4 × 15ml spoons/
  4 tablespoons flaked
  almonds

Remove the coarse stems from the watercress to give about 75g/3 oz leaves and fine stems. Blanch in boiling water for 1 minute.

Tip any excess liquid from the cheese then sieve the cheese.

Drain and refresh the watercress under cold running water. Drain well, pressing out as much excess water as possible. Chop finely.

Mix the watercress, cheese, ground almonds, salt and pepper.

Season the trout and squeeze lemon juice in the cavity.

Divide the filling between the trout, then fold the flap of skin over it to hold the filling in. Lay in a frying pan or shallow flameproof dish that is just large enough to hold them in a single layer.

Place over a moderate heat for 2 minutes, then add the wine, adjust the heat so the wine barely bubbles, cover tightly and cook for about 15 minutes until the trout are tender.

Meanwhile, lightly toast the almonds.

Carefully transfer the trout to a warmed plate. Add the almonds to the pan or dish, increase the heat and cook, stirring, until the liquid has almost evaporated.

Serve the trout with the nuts and remaining liquid spooned over.

SOLE WITH SCALLOPS AND CORAL SAUCE

 25 minutes

4 large fillets of sole, skinned
salt, freshly ground white
  pepper
juice and rind of ½ lemon
4 scallops
15ml spoon/1 tablespoon
  finely chopped chives
5 × 15ml spoons/
  5 tablespoons crème fraîche
  or *double cream, whipped*
300ml/½ pint fish stock

FOR THE GARNISH

sprigs of chervil or *parsley*

Place each fillet between 2 pieces of greaseproof paper, then flatten them slightly with a rolling pin. Season with salt and pepper and sprinkle with lemon juice.

Separate the corals from the bodies of the scallops. Place one body on each fillet.

Fold the chives, lemon rind and salt and pepper to taste into 4 × 15ml spoons/4 tablespoons of the crème fraîche or cream and place on the scallops.

Fold the sole over the scallops to make a parcel and secure the edges with a cocktail stick.

Bring half the stock to just below simmering point in a shallow pan that the fish will just fit. Gently lower in the sole parcels, cover with greaseproof paper and poach for 5 minutes.

Meanwhile poach the scallop corals gently for a bare 30 seconds in the remaining stock. Remove the corals with a perforated spoon and purée with the remaining crème fraîche or cream and stock. Pass through a sieve if liked.

Remove the fillets using a fish slice and keep warm.

Add the stock used for poaching the corals to the pan and boil until reduced to 3 × 15ml spoons/3 tablespoons. Remove from the heat and stir in the coral purée. Season to taste and pass through a sieve, if liked. Divide between 4 warmed plates.

Remove the cocktail sticks from the fish and place the sole on the sauce. Garnish with sprigs of chervil or parsley.

SEAFOOD LASAGNE

 10 minutes + 45 minutes cooking, then resting

200ml/7 fl oz single or double
  cream
1 egg, beaten
1 egg yolk
salt, freshly ground black
  pepper
10ml spoon/2 teaspoons finely
  chopped dill
100g/4 oz fresh lasagne verde
6 clams
100g/4 oz peeled prawns
18 mussels, shelled
75g/3 oz monkfish fillet, cut
  into 2.5cm/1 inch cubes
flesh of 3 tomatoes, chopped
15g/½ oz freshly grated
  Parmesan cheese
15g/½ oz unsalted butter

Bring the cream to simmering point, then stir into the egg and egg yolk. Season well with salt and pepper and add the dill.

Place a layer of overlapping pieces of lasagne in the bottom of a buttered shallow ovenproof dish. Cover with the clams, prawns, mussels and monkfish. Pour the cream over and cover with the tomatoes.

Cover with the remaining lasagne, sprinkle the Parmesan over and dot with the butter.

Cook in a moderate oven, 180°C/350°F/Gas 4, for about 40 minutes until the centre is just set. Place under a hot grill to brown the top, if necessary.

Leave to stand for a few minutes before cutting into 4 square or rectangular portions and carefully transferring to warmed serving plates.

Note: Dried lasagne can be used if fresh is not available. Check the packet to see if it has to be boiled first.

SALMON WITH RED VERMOUTH SAUCE

 15 minutes

4 fillets of salmon, skinned
salt, freshly ground white
   pepper

FOR THE SAUCE

150ml/¼ pint fish stock
150ml/¼ pint red vermouth
1 clove
4 juniper berries, crushed
1 small bay leaf, broken
small sprig of thyme
15ml spoon/1 tablespoon
   orange rind
15ml spoon/1 tablespoon
   lemon rind
15g/½ oz unsalted butter,
   diced

FOR THE GARNISH

fine strips of blanched orange
   and lemon rind

Simmer the first 8 ingredients for the sauce together for 10 minutes, then boil until reduced to 150ml/5 fl oz.

Meanwhile, steam the salmon for 3–4 minutes.

Over a low heat, gradually swirl the butter into the sauce. Season the sauce and the salmon with salt and pepper.

Spoon the sauce over warmed plates. Place the salmon on top and garnish with strips of orange and lemon rind.

POACHED TURBOT WITH CORIANDER AND CREAM SAUCE

 15 minutes

50ml/2 fl oz dry vermouth
75ml/3 fl oz full-bodied dry
   white wine
175ml/6 fl oz fish stock
15ml spoon/1 tablespoon
   lightly toasted crushed
   coriander seeds
strip of lemon peel
salt, freshly ground white
   pepper
4 fillets of turbot, about
   150g/5oz each
50ml/2 fl oz double cream

FOR THE GARNISH

fresh coriander or parsley

Gently heat the vermouth, wine, stock, corriander seeds, lemon peel, salt and pepper to simmering point in a frying pan that is just large enough to hold the fish in a single layer.

Add the fish, reduce the heat so the liquid barely moves and cook for about 4 minutes.

Transfer the fish to a warmed plate with a fish slice, cover and keep warm.

Boil the poaching liquid until reduced to 75ml/3 fl oz. Stir in the cream and boil briefly. Remove the coriander seeds and lemon peel with a perforated spoon.

Spoon some of the sauce onto 4 warmed plates. Place the fish on top and garnish with fresh coriander or parsley.

SEAFOOD BROCHETTES WITH COCONUT SAUCE

  20 minutes

50g/2 oz creamed coconut
1 small onion, finely chopped
5ml spoon/1 teaspoon
   turmeric
5ml spoon/1 teaspoon ground
   cumin
5ml spoon/1 teaspoon ground
   coriander
1.25ml spoon/¼ teaspoon
   cayenne pepper
50g/2 oz cashew nuts, chopped
salt
5ml spoon/1 teaspoon lemon
   juice
approx 550g/1¼ lb prepared
   mixed fish, eg turbot,
   monkfish, clams, salmon,
   cut into cubes
12–16 seedless black grapes
8 lychees, stoned and halved
40g/1½ oz unsalted butter,
   melted
juice of 1 lime

Blend the coconut with 175ml/5 fl oz water, then mix with the onion and spices in a saucepan, bring to the boil, stir in the nuts and simmer for about 5 minutes, stirring occasionally.

Purée in a blender, add salt and lemon juice to taste, return to the rinsed pan and keep warm.

Thread the fish, grapes and lychees onto skewers. Mix the butter and lime juice together and brush over the fish.

Grill the fish for about 4 minutes, brushing occasionally with the butter and lime juice, until just tender.

Serve accompanied by the warm sauce.

SALMON WITH LEMON BALM AND VANILLA SAUCE

  20 minutes

½ vanilla pod, split
250ml/8 fl oz full-bodied dry
   white wine
salt, freshly ground white
   pepper
4 fillets of salmon, about
   175g/6 oz each
8 lemon balm leaves
4 sprigs lemon balm
8 sorrel leaves
75g/3 oz unsalted butter,
   diced
lemon juice

FOR THE GARNISH

lemon balm

Gently simmer the vanilla pod in the wine for about 10 minutes.

Meanwhile, season the salmon and place 2 lemon balm leaves on each piece.

Place the sprigs of lemon balm in a steaming basket, lay a piece of salmon on each sprig and steam for about 10 minutes, until the fish is just cooked.

Meanwhile, blanch the sorrel leaves for 1 minute, then refresh under cold running water. Dry well. Place in the steaming basket to warm.

Boil the wine until reduced to 3 × 15ml spoons/3 tablespoons. Lower the heat, remove the vanilla pod, then gradually whisk in the butter making sure that each piece is completely incorporated before adding the next. Season with salt, pepper and lemon juice.

Place 2 sorrel leaves on each of 4 plates. Discard the lemon balm sprigs from beneath the salmon and place the fish on top of the sorrel. Spoon the sauce around or over and garnish with fresh lemon balm.

FETTUCINE WITH A DUO OF SALMON

 20 minutes

50g/2 oz unsalted butter
225g/8 oz skinned salmon
* fillet, cut into 5cm/½ inch*
* dice*
3 × 15ml spoons/
* 3 tablespoons finely*
* chopped shallot*
flesh of 2 tomatoes, chopped
100ml/4 fl oz medium-bodied
* dry white wine*
175ml/6 fl oz fish stock
175ml/6 fl oz double cream
5 × 15ml spoons/
* 5 tablespoons finely*
* chopped basil*
350g/12 oz fresh fettucine or
* 300g/10 oz dried fettucine*
* (see Note)*
100g/4 oz thinly sliced smoked
* salmon, cut into strips*
salt, freshly ground black
* pepper*

Heat the butter in a frying pan over a moderate heat, add the fresh salmon and cook, stirring frequently, for 30 seconds.

Remove with a perforated spoon.

Add the shallot and tomato flesh to the pan and cook for 2 minutes, stirring occasionally.

Stir the wine and stock into the shallot and tomato mixture and boil over a high heat until syrupy. Stir in the cream and basil and boil until slightly thickened.

Remove the pan from the heat.

Cook the fresh pasta in boiling salted water for 1–2 minutes until just tender, but still firm to the bite.

Drain the pasta well and keep warm.

Quickly bring the sauce back to the boil. Add the diced salmon, then remove from the heat. Stir in the smoked salmon. Season to taste.

Mound the fettucine on four warmed plates, making a small well in the centre of each mound. Divide the salmon and sauce between the mounds. Finish with basil leaves, if liked.

Note: If fresh fettucine is not available, dried can be used. Start cooking it while the shallots are cooking and cook for the length of time given on the packet.

SOLE WITH CUCUMBER MOUSSE

  15 minutes + 12–15 minutes cooking

175g/6 oz cucumber, peeled
* and finely chopped*
2 × 15ml spoons/
2 tablespoons finely chopped
* shallot*
4 large fillets of sole
salt, freshly ground white
* pepper*
40g/1½ oz full fat soft cheese
3 small egg whites
2 × 15ml spoons/
2 tablespoons finely chopped
* fennel*
50ml/2 fl oz medium-bodied
* dry white wine*
15g/½ oz unsalted butter

Cook the cucumber with the shallot and 3 × 15ml spoons/ 3 tablespoons water in a covered saucepan until softened and the excess liquid has evaporated.

Meanwhile, place the sole fillets individually between 2 sheets of greaseproof paper or clingfilm and beat to flatten them out.

Purée the cucumber, then return to the pan and heat again to drive off any excess liquid. Remove from the heat and beat in the salt, pepper and cheese.

Whisk the egg whites until stiff but not dry and fold into the cucumber mixture with the fennel.

Season the fillets. Place the cucumber mixture on half of each fillet, then fold the fillets over the filling. Carefully transfer to a shallow buttered ovenproof dish. Pour the wine around and place in a moderate oven, 180°C/350°F/Gas 4, for 12–15 minutes.

Carefully transfer the fish to warmed plates. Bring the cooking juices to the boil, and boil until slightly reduced. Reduce the heat to very low and swirl in the butter. Season and spoon around the fish.

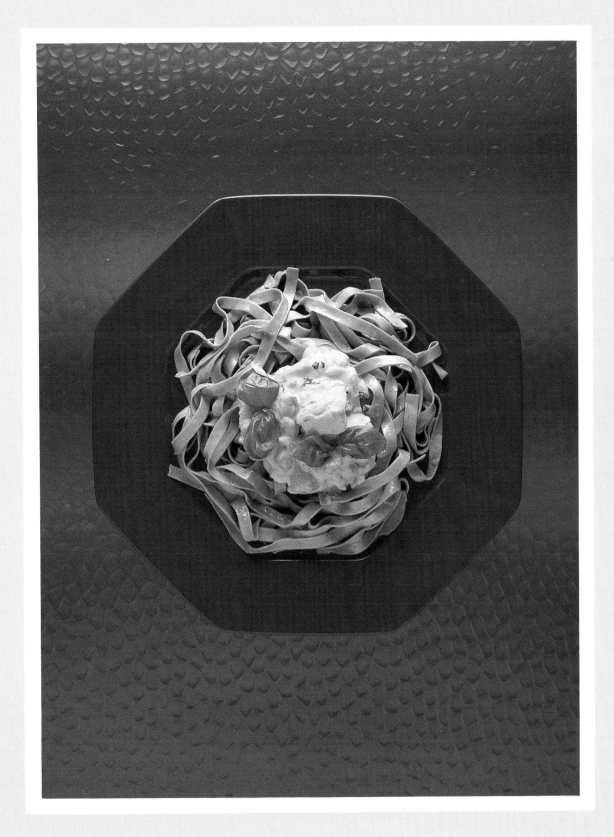

FETTUCINE WITH
A DUO OF SALMON

59

POULTRY

Chicken breasts with parsley
Breasts of chicken with lime
Breasts of duck with passionfruit
Chicken strips with walnuts
Duck with lemon and caraway
Chicken with courgettes and almonds
Tea-scented duck breasts with vanilla sauce
Honeyed duck with lime and herbs
Duck with apple and mint compote
Saffron and wine glazed chicken
Turkey with capers and cream
Chicken breasts with artichoke and lemon sauce
Chicken baked with limes and yoghurt
Grilled quail with bay leaves and sausage
Chicken with red peppers
Poussins with fresh fig stuffing

CHICKEN BREASTS WITH PARSLEY

 15 minutes

65g/2½ oz unsalted butter
15ml spoon/1 tablespoon olive
  oil
4 chicken breasts, skinned and
  split into 2 lengthways
salt and freshly ground black
  pepper
3 × 15ml spoons/
  3 tablespoons lemon juice
3 × 15ml spoons/
  3 tablespoons chopped
  parsley

FOR THE GARNISH

1 lemon, thinly sliced

Heat 40g/1½ oz butter in a large frying pan with the oil. Add the chicken in a single layer and cook over a moderately high heat for about 2–3 minutes each side.

Transfer to a warmed plate using a slotted spoon, season with salt and pepper and keep warm.

Stir the lemon juice into the pan, dislodging the sediment, lower the heat and stir in the parsley and remaining butter.

Return the breasts to the pan and turn them over in the sauce.

Serve topped with slices of lemon.

BREASTS OF CHICKEN WITH LIME

 15 minutes

4 chicken breasts
salt, freshly ground black
  pepper
olive oil
2 limes
15ml spoon/1 tablespoon
  tarragon mustard (or see
  page 00)
15ml spoon/1 tablespoon
  single-flower honey
5ml spoon/1 teaspoon toasted
  coriander seeds, crushed

Season the chicken breasts with salt and pepper, then brush with oil. Grill for about 2 minutes each side.

Meanwhile, peel and thinly slice the limes. Mix together the mustard, honey and coriander seeds.

Place the breasts in a buttered shallow ovenproof dish and spread the mustard mixture over. Cover with slices of lime and place in a moderately hot oven, 190°C/375°F/Gas 5, for about 7 minutes.

Serve with the juices spooned over.

BREASTS OF DUCK WITH PASSIONFRUIT

 15 minutes

2 large passionfruit
nutmeg
4 duck breasts, skinned
salt, freshly ground black
    pepper
freshly ground white pepper
caster sugar, optional

FOR THE GARNISH

sprigs of chervil
long thin strips of orange rind

Cut the passionfruit in half, reserve a few of the seeds and scoop the remainder into a sieve, then rub the pulp and juice through.

Grate a little nutmeg over the duck, then place under a hot grill, skinned side uppermost, for 3 minutes.

Turn the duck over with tongs and grill for a further 3 minutes. Transfer to a warmed plate, season lightly with salt and freshly ground black pepper and keep warm.

Gently warm the passionfruit juice in a small saucepan. Season lightly with salt and freshly ground white pepper and add a little sugar if the juice is too sharp.

Carve the duck into slices and arrange in fan shapes on warmed plates. Spoon the juice around and garnish with chervil and strips of orange rind.

CHICKEN STRIPS WITH WALNUTS

 15–20 minutes

5 × 15ml spoons/
    5 tablespoons whisky
approx 2 × 15ml spoons/
    2 tablespoons mustard
    powder
450g/1 lb chicken breasts,
    skinned and cut into
    2.5cm/½ inch strips
100g/4 oz walnuts, very finely
    chopped
75g/3oz unsalted butter
1 garlic clove, crushed
3 × 15ml spoons/
    3 tablespoons lemon juice
salt, freshly ground black
    pepper

Blend 15ml/1 tablespoon whisky into the mustard powder. Spread over the strips of chicken. If time permits, leave to marinate for at least 15 minutes.

Roll the strips in the nuts to coat them evenly.

Press the nuts firmly into the strips.

Heat the butter in a frying pan, add the garlic and chicken strips and cook over a moderate heat for about 4 minutes, turning the strips so they brown evenly.

Transfer the chicken to a warmed plate and keep warm.

Stir the remaining whisky and the lemon juice into the pan and boil for a minute or two. Season with salt and pepper and spoon over the chicken.

DUCK WITH LEMON AND CARAWAY

 15–20 minutes

4 duck breasts
5ml spoon/1 teaspoon
   caraway seeds, chopped
200ml/7 fl oz lemon juice
225ml/8 fl oz chicken stock
approx 40g/1½ oz unsalted
   butter, diced
4 × 5ml spoons/4 teaspoons
   caster sugar
salt, freshly ground black
   pepper

FOR THE GARNISH

fine strips of lemon rind,
   blanched
sprigs of dill

Gently ease the skin away from the duck breasts, leaving it intact around the edges. Insert a few caraway seeds between the breast and skin.

Place the duck, skin-side down, in a hot frying pan, and cook over a high heat for 2-3 minutes until the fat begins to run. Turn the duck over with tongs, reduce the heat slightly and cook for a further 2 minutes.

Pour off the surplus fat, reduce the heat, add the lemon juice, adjust the heat so that the liquid just simmers, cover and cook for 2-3 minutes. The meat should be pink inside.

Transfer the duck to a warmed plate and keep warm.

Boil the lemon juice until it has almost evaporated, then stir in the stock and remaining caraway seeds and simmer until reduced to about 150ml/5 fl oz.

Reduce the heat then gradually whisk in the butter, making sure each piece is fully incorporated before adding the next. Add sugar and seasoning to taste, then keep warm over a low heat. Do not allow the sauce to boil.

Remove the skin from the duck breasts, then either leave them whole or cut into slices. Place on 4 warmed plates and spoon the sauce over. Garnish with the lemon rind and sprigs of dill.

CHICKEN WITH COURGETTES AND ALMONDS

 20 minutes

10ml spoon/2 teaspoons
   cornflour
2 × 15ml spoons/
   2 tablespoons soy sauce
2 × 5ml spoons/2 teaspoons
   brown sugar
salt, freshly ground black
   pepper
4 chicken breasts, skinned and
   cut into thin strips
2 × 15ml spoons/
   2 tablespoons sesame oil
75g/3 oz split almonds
4 spring onions, cut into strips
225g/8 oz small courgettes,
   cut into long matchsticks
3 × 15 ml spoons/
   3 tablespoons saké or fino
   sherry

Blend the cornflour, soy sauce, sugar, salt and pepper together in a bowl. Stir in the chicken to coat it well.

Heat the oil in a large, heavy non-stick frying pan or wok, add the almonds and cook over a moderate heat, stirring frequently, until browned. Remove with a perforated spoon and drain on absorbent paper.

Lift the chicken out of the soy sauce mixture and add to the pan. Cook over a high heat, stirring, until evenly browned.

Stir in the spring onions and courgettes and cook over a moderate heat for about 3 minutes, stirring occasionally.

Blend the saké or sherry into the remaining soy sauce mixture, then stir into the pan. Bring to the boil, stirring, add the almonds and simmer briefly until slightly thickened.

TEA-SCENTED DUCK BREASTS
WITH VANILLA SAUCE

TEA-SCENTED DUCK BREASTS WITH VANILLA SAUCE

 15–20 minutes

4 duck breasts
5 × 5ml spoons/5 teaspoons
 orange Pekoe tea
salt, freshly ground black
 pepper
50ml/2 fl oz white wine
 vinegar
2 × 15ml spoons/
 2 tablespoons clear honey
425ml/15 fl oz chicken stock
½ vanilla pod, split
15ml spoon/1 tablespoon
 unsalted butter, diced

TO SERVE

curly endive and spring onion
 salad

Place the duck, skin-side uppermost, in the top part of a steamer. Place over 300ml/½ pint boiling water, to which the tea has been added, cover and steam for 6 minutes.

Skin the duck, then place skinned side uppermost under a very hot grill for 3 minutes. Turn it over and grill for 2 minutes. Season with salt and pepper and leave in a warm place for a few minutes.

Meanwhile, boil the vinegar and honey together in a heavy saucepan until syrupy and just beginning to caramelize. Remove from the heat immediately. Stir in the stock, add the vanilla pod, then simmer until reduced by half.

Reduce the heat beneath the sauce, remove the vanilla pod and swirl in the butter. Adjust the seasoning.

Cut the duck into slices. Spoon the sauce over four warmed plates and arrange the duck slices in a fan shape on the sauce.

Serve with a side salad of curly endive and spring onions.

HONEYED DUCK WITH LIME AND HERBS

  20 minutes

4 × 15ml spoons/
 4 tablespoons lime juice
3 × 15ml spoons/
 3 tablespoons clear honey
4 duck breasts
7.5ml spoon/½ tablespoon very
 finely chopped rosemary
15ml spoon/1 tablespoon
 finely chopped marjoram
15ml spoon/1 tablespoon
 finely chopped thyme
salt, freshly ground black
 pepper
7g/¼ oz unsalted butter

FOR THE GARNISH

slices of lime

Blend the lime juice with the honey. Prick the duck skins and spread some of the mixture over the breasts.

Mix the herbs with salt and press into the breasts.

Place skin-side up under a hot grill for about 4 minutes, brushing once with the honey mixture, taking care not to dislodge the herbs. Turn the breasts over, brush with the honey mixture again, taking care not to dislodge the herbs, and grill for about another 3 minutes.

Meanwhile, gently warm the remaining honey mixture, season lightly and swirl in the butter. Keep warm but do not allow to boil.

Remove the skin from the breasts then cut them into slices, if liked. Divide the sauce between 4 warmed plates and place the breasts on top. Garnish with slices of lime.

DUCK WITH APPLE AND MINT COMPOTE

 20 minutes

50ml/2 fl oz lemon juice
225ml/8 fl oz medium-bodied dry white wine
40g/1½ oz sugar
550g/1¼ lb crisp, tart apples, peeled, cored and cut into 2.5cm/1 inch slices
2 × 15ml spoons/ 2 tablespoons finely chopped fresh mint
4 duck breasts
salt, freshly ground black pepper

FOR THE GARNISH

small sprigs of mint leaves

Gently heat the lemon juice, wine and sugar together in a large frying pan or wide saucepan, stirring, until the sugar has dissolved, then increase the heat and bring to the boil.

Add the apples to the liquid, lower the heat and cook gently until the apples are just tender – about 5–7 minutes. Carefully remove the apples slices with a perforated spoon and place in a bowl.

Bring the liquid to the boil and boil until reduced by half. Pour over the apple slices and carefully stir in the mint. Cover and leave for the flavours to mingle slightly.

Cook the duck breasts, skin side uppermost, under a fairly hot grill for 3 minutes. Turn the breasts over and cook for 3 minutes then turn them over again and cook the skin side for 1 more minute. Season with salt and pepper.

Transfer the duck breasts to warmed plates and place some of the apple and mint compote, with some of the juices, alongside. Garnish the duck with small sprigs of mint.

SAFFRON AND WINE GLAZED CHICKEN

 25 minutes

pinch of saffron threads
225ml/8 fl oz full-bodied dry white wine
100ml/4 fl oz dry vermouth
4 chicken breasts
300ml/½ pint chicken stock
50g/2 oz unsalted butter, diced
salt, freshly ground white pepper

Blend together the saffron, wine and vermouth in a frying pan that the chicken breasts will just fit. Heat gently to simmering point.

Remove the skin from the chicken. Stir the saffron liquid then place the chicken breasts in it, cover and poach for about 5 minutes, depending on size.

Boil the stock until reduced to 100ml/4 fl oz.

Turn the chicken over and cook for another 5 minutes or so.

Transfer the chicken to a warmed plate, cover and keep warm.

Boil the poaching liquor until reduced to 2 × 15ml spoons/ 2 tablespoons.

Stir the stock into the wine and reduce to 75ml/3 fl oz. Reduce the heat and gradually swirl in the butter, making sure each piece is fully incorporated before adding the next. Season with salt and pepper.

Meanwhile, slice the chicken breasts, re-form and keep warm.

Place the chicken on 4 warmed plates and spoon the sauce over. Pass it through a sieve at the same time to remove the saffron threads, if liked.

DUCK WITH
APPLE AND MINT COMPOTE

TURKEY WITH CAPERS AND CREAM

  20–25 minutes

25g/1 oz unsalted butter
2 × 15ml spoons/
  2 tablespoons olive oil
4 turkey fillets
2 small shallots
salt, freshly ground black
  pepper
100ml/4 fl oz chicken stock
50ml/2 fl oz dry vermouth
15ml spoon/1 tablespoon
  lemon juice
75ml/3 fl oz whipping cream
2 × 15ml spoons/
  2 tablespoons capers
15ml spoon/1 tablespoon
  chopped tarragon

FOR THE GARNISH

sprigs of parsley

Heat the butter and oil in a heavy-based frying pan, add the turkey and cook for about 3 minutes each side. Chop the shallots.

Season the turkey with salt and pepper, then transfer to a warmed dish with a perforated spoon and keep warm.

Pour all but 1½ × 15ml spoons/1½ tablespoons of the fat from the pan then stir in the shallots and cook for 2 minutes.

Stir in the stock, vermouth and lemon juice and boil until reduced to about 75ml/3 fl oz. Stir in the cream and capers and simmer until slightly thickened.

Meanwhile, cut the turkey into slices. Re-form and keep warm. Spoon the sauce over 4 warmed plates and sprinkle the chopped tarragon over. Arrange the slices of turkey in the sauce and garnish with sprigs of parsley.

Alternatively, place the fillets, whole, on warmed plates, spoon the sauce over and sprinkle with the chopped tarragon. Garnish the edge of the sauce with the sprigs of parsley.

CHICKEN BREASTS WITH ARTICHOKES AND LEMON SAUCE

  30 minutes

1 large artichoke
lemon juice
salt, freshly ground black
  pepper
4 chicken breasts
100ml/4 fl oz medium-bodied
  dry white wine
175ml/6 fl oz crème fraîche
freshly ground white pepper

FOR THE GARNISH

sprigs of chervil

Cut the artichokes into quarters then, working quickly as the cut surfaces soon discolour, cut out the hairy choke. Place the quarters immediately in a saucepan of simmering salted water, acidulated with lemon juice. Cook for 12–15 minutes until tender.

Meanwhile, season the chicken breasts with salt and black pepper and grill, skin-side up, for about 4 minutes. Turn them over with tongs and grill on the other side for 4 minutes.

Boil the wine until reduced to 15ml/1 tablespoon.

When the artichoke is cooked, drain well, cut away the base and put in a blender. Scrape the flesh from the base of the largest leaves and add to the blender. Reserve some of the smaller leaves for garnish. Add a little of the crème fraîche and 5ml/1 teaspoon lemon juice and purée until smooth.

When the wine has reduced, stir in the remaining crème fraîche and boil until reduced to 100ml/4 fl oz. Whisk in the artichoke purée and heat through gently. Season with salt and white pepper.

Remove the skin from the breasts and either serve them whole or cut into thin slices. Spoon the sauce onto 4 warmed plates, place the chicken breasts on top and garnish with artichoke leaves and chervil.

TURKEY WITH CAPERS
AND CREAM

CHICKEN BAKED WITH LIMES AND YOGHURT

 10 minutes + 30 minutes cooking

4 chicken breasts, skinned
2 limes
2 × 15ml spoons/
   2 tablespoons dry vermouth
50g/2 oz soft cheese
150ml/5 fl oz plain yoghurt
salt, freshly ground black
   pepper
5ml spoon/1 teaspoon finely
   chopped fresh marjoram
5ml spoon/1 teaspoon sesame
   seeds

FOR THE GARNISH

fresh coriander or parsley

Cook the chicken breasts in a non-stick frying pan over a moderate heat for 30 seconds each side.

Meanwhile, grate the rind finely from the limes, then squeeze out the juice. Mix the juice with the vermouth.

Beat the rind into the cheese with the yoghurt, salt and pepper, then add the marjoram.

Place the chicken breasts in a shallow ovenproof dish that is large enough to hold them in a single layer. Sprinkle half the lime juice mixture over the breasts, turn them over and sprinkle with the remaining juice. Spoon the yoghurt mixture over the chicken, cover with a lid or foil and bake in a moderate oven, 180°C/350°F/Gas 4, for 30–35 minutes.

Meanwhile, heat the sesame seeds in a heavy bottomed, non-stick pan over a moderate heat until lightly toasted.

Transfer the chicken breasts to a warmed serving dish, whisk the cooking juices to blend them together, then spoon over the chicken. Sprinkle the sesame seeds over the top. Place leaves of fresh coriander or parsley around the edge of the dish.

GRILLED QUAIL WITH BAY LEAVES AND SAUSAGE

 35 minutes

15g/½ oz dried chanterelle or
   other wild mushrooms,
   chopped
1 shallot, finely chopped
9 juniper berries, crushed
2 bay leaves, broken
pinch of freshly grated nutmeg
pinch of cinnamon
75ml/3 fl oz dark rum
400ml/14 fl oz fruity,
   medium-bodied red wine
100g/4 oz unsalted butter
8 quails
8 small pieces bread
8 bay leaves
225g/8 oz fresh sausage
approx 10ml spoon/
   2 teaspoons redcurrant jelly
salt, freshly ground black
   pepper

Soak the mushrooms in 75ml/3 fl oz hot water for 5 minutes.

Meanwhile, set the next 7 ingredients to simmer together until reduced to about 175ml/6 fl oz.

Drain the mushrooms, squeezing out as much liquor as possible, add to the simmering liquid, then mix with half of the butter.

Place equal amounts of the mixture inside each quail. Plug the cavity with a piece of bread.

Soften the bay leaves in warm water. Cut the sausage into 8 pieces.

Thread one bay leaf onto each of 4 skewers, followed by a quail, threaded crossways, then a piece of sausage, also threaded crossways. Repeat.

Brush liberally with some of the simmering liquid, then grill, frequently turning and brushing with the liquid, for about 10 minutes.

Meanwhile, strain the liquid, if liked, for a really smooth sauce, and reheat in a clean pan.

Stir redcurrant jelly to taste into the liquid, then, over a very low heat, gradually whisk in the remaining butter, making sure each piece is fully incorporated before adding the next. Season with salt and pepper.

Put 2 quails and 2 pieces of sausage on each plate and spoon the sauce over.

GRILLED QUAIL
WITH BAY LEAVES
AND SAUSAGE

71

CHICKEN WITH RED PEPPERS

 15 minutes + 20–25 minutes cooking

15g/½ oz unsalted butter
2 × 15ml spoons/
  2 tablespoons olive oil
4 chicken breasts
4 small or 3 large red peppers
salt, freshly ground black
  pepper
200ml/7 fl oz medium-bodied
  dry white wine
sprig of marjoram

Heat the butter and oil in a frying pan large enough to hold the chicken in a single layer.

Add the chicken breasts, skin side down and cook over a moderately high heat until lightly browned.

Lower the heat slightly, turn the breasts over with tongs and cook for 3–4 minutes.

Meanwhile, seed the peppers and cut into thin strips.

Add the seasoning, peppers, wine and marjoram, bring to the boil, cover tightly and cook gently for 20–25 minutes.

Remove the chicken and simmer the contents of the frying pan, if necessary, to evaporate excess moisture.

Remove the sprig of marjoram and serve the chicken breasts on a bed of red peppers.

POUSSINS WITH FRESH FIG STUFFING

  25 minutes + 25 minutes cooking

small pinch of saffron threads
6 × 15 ml spoons/
  6 tablespoons bulgur
salt, freshly ground black
  pepper
4 black figs
4 poussins, about 350g/12 oz
  each
25ml/1 fl oz dry oloroso, if
  available
175ml/6 fl oz dessert wine (or
  200ml/7 fl oz if dry oloroso
  is not used)
300ml/½ pint chicken stock
2 × 15ml spoons/
  2 tablespoons cognac

Sprinkle the saffron onto the bulgur, add the salt and pepper, then stir in 200ml/7 fl oz boiling water. Leave for 5 minutes, until all the water has been absorbed.

Meanwhile, chop the figs and season the poussins inside and out. Stir the bulgur, then mix in the figs. Divide between the cavities in the poussins. Secure the openings with skewers or sew them up. Cook in a non-stick frying pan for about 8–10 minutes, turning them over so they brown lightly and evenly.

Transfer the poussins to a roasting tin and cook in a moderately hot oven, 220°C/425°F/Gas 7, for about 25 minutes, until the skin is crisp and golden and the juices between the legs and body run clear.

Meanwhile, boil the oloroso, if used, and the wine in the frying pan until reduced to 25ml/1 fl oz. Stir in the stock and reduce to 150ml/5 fl oz.

Transfer the poussins to a warmed plate using a spatula or fish slice, and keep warm.

Pour any excess fat from the roasting tin, stir in the cognac and boil until almost evaporated. Stir in the reduced stock, bring back to the boil and adjust the seasoning.

Meanwhile, remove the trussing string and skewers, if used. Spoon the stuffing onto 4 warmed plates. Spoon a little of the sauce onto the stuffing. Place the poussins beside the stuffing and spoon the remaining sauce around the birds.

MEAT

Noisettes of lamb with tomato and mint vinaigrette
Kidneys with gin and juniper
Beef with water chestnuts and green peppercorns
Kidneys with sage and prosciutto
Fillets of beef with mustard butter
Escalopes of calves liver with smooth shallot sauce
Steak with buttered spring onions and parsley
Beefburgers with mushrooms
Noisettes of lamb with herb sauce
Pork with Pernod and apricots
Italian veal
Veal balls with gooseberry sauce
Crispy pork in apple batter
Fillet of lamb baked in salt with herbs
Veal with light lettuce soufflé stuffing
Veal with cucumber and mangetout peas
Sliced pork in spiced milk
'Boiled' beef with carrots, parsley dumplings and gravy
Mini racks of lamb with creamy ham and mushroom stuffing
Beef with lovage
Pork with grapes and chestnuts
Lamb with olives and lemon

NOISETTES OF LAMB WITH TOMATO AND MINT VINAIGRETTE

 10 minutes

50ml/2 fl oz olive oil
2 × 15ml spoons/
   2 tablespoons chopped mint
15ml spoon/1 tablespoon lime
   juice
10ml spoon/2 teaspoons finely
   chopped parsley
3 × 15ml spoons/
   3 tablespoons chopped
   shallot
flesh of 4 ripe tomatoes,
   chopped
salt, freshly ground black
   pepper
40g/1½ oz unsalted butter,
   diced
8 noisettes of lamb

FOR THE GARNISH

sprigs of mint

Mix the first 7 ingredients together in a bowl.

Heat the butter in a frying pan, add the noisettes and cook for about 3 minutes each side.

Meanwhile, place the bowl of vinaigrette over a saucepan of hot water and warm through, stirring frequently.

Remove the noisettes from the pan using a fork and drain on absorbent paper.

Spoon some of the sauce over 4 warmed plates, place the lamb on top and spoon the remaining sauce over. Garnish with sprigs of mint.

KIDNEYS WITH GIN AND JUNIPER

 15 minutes

40g/1½ oz unsalted butter
8 lambs kidneys, cut into
   halves, cores removed
50ml/2 fl oz gin
15ml spoon/1 tablespoon
   crushed juniper berries
salt and freshly ground black
   pepper
4 × 15ml spoons/
   4 tablespoons soured cream

FOR THE GARNISH

sprigs of parsley

Heat the butter in a frying pan, add the kidneys and cook over a fairly high heat, stirring occasionally, to seal the outsides and lightly brown them. Stir in the gin and juniper berries and boil for a few seconds.

Season with salt and pepper, then stir in the soured cream to coat the kidneys.

Serve immediately garnished with parsley.

NOISETTES OF LAMB
WITH TOMATO AND MINT
VINAIGRETTE

BEEF WITH WATER CHESTNUTS AND GREEN PEPPERCORNS

 15 minutes

50g/2 oz butter
2 shallots, finely chopped
550g/1¼ lb topside of beef
75g/3 oz fresh shiitake
  mushrooms
8 canned water chestnuts,
  halved
2 × 5ml spoons/2 teaspoons
  green peppercorns
4 × 15ml spoons/
  4 tablespoons red wine
2 × 15ml spoons/
  2 tablespoons red vermouth
salt, freshly ground black
  pepper

FOR THE GARNISH

watercress leaves

Melt the butter in a large frying pan, add the shallots and cook over a low heat for about 5 minutes until softened.

Meanwhile, cut the beef into 2cm/¾ inch cubes. Stir the beef into the frying pan and cook over a moderately high heat for 2–3 minutes, stirring frequently.

Meanwhile, stem the mushrooms, cut the caps into slices and chop the stems finely. Stir the mushrooms, water chestnuts and green peppercorns into the pan and cook for 1 minute.

Add the wine, vermouth, salt and pepper and allow to boil for 2–3 minutes until the waterchestnuts are heated through and the liquid reduced slightly. Serve garnished with watercress leaves.

Note: Shiitake mushrooms are now being cultivated in Europe and are available fresh from good greengrocers and supermarkets. Dried shiitake mushrooms, available from oriental food shops and good grocers, can be substituted, but the flavour and texture of the dish will be altered. The same applies to other dried mushrooms, wild mushrooms or large flat mushrooms.

If you can't get fresh shiitake, use 25g/1 oz dried shiitake, cover with boiling water and leave for 20 minutes. Squeeze dry.

KIDNEYS WITH SAGE AND PROSCIUTTO

 15 minutes

15ml spoon/1 tablespoon
unsalted butter
15ml spoon/1 tablespoon olive
oil
8 lambs kidneys, halved and
cored
3 × 15ml spoons/
3 tablespoons finely
chopped shallots
150ml/¼ pint full-bodied dry
white wine
225ml/8 fl oz veal or chicken
stock
8 small sage leaves
50g/2 oz prosciutto, thinly
sliced and cut into strips
salt, freshly ground black
pepper

FOR THE GARNISH

very small sage leaves

Heat the butter and oil in a frying pan, add the kidneys and cook over a moderately high heat for about 2 minutes, stirring occasionally.

Transfer to a warmed plate with a perforated spoon. Cover.

Add the shallots to the pan and cook for about 3 minutes over a moderate heat, stirring occasionally. Stir in the wine and boil until about 2 × 15ml spoons/2 tablespoons are left. Stir in the stock and sage and boil until reduced to about 150ml/5 fl oz.

Add the prosciutto, return the kidneys to the pan, season lightly and heat gently for about 2 minutes. Lift out the kidneys and most of the prosciutto with a perforated spoon. Divide the sauce between 4 warmed plates, place the kidneys and prosciutto on top and garnish with additional very small sage leaves.

FILLETS OF BEEF WITH MUSTARD BUTTER

 15 minutes

215g/7½ oz unsalted butter,
diced
4 fillet steaks, about
150–175g/5–6 oz each
3 × 15ml spoons/
3 tablespoons finely
chopped shallot
3 × 15ml spoons/
3 tablespoons tarragon
mustard
3 × 15ml spoons/
3 tablespoons mustard seeds
3 × 15ml spoons/
3 tablespoons finely
chopped thyme
3 × 15ml spoons/
3 tablespoons finely
chopped parsley
salt, freshly ground black
pepper

Heat 40g/1½ oz butter in a large frying pan, add the steaks and cook for 2–3 minutes each side. Transfer the steaks to a warmed plate with tongs, cover and keep warm. Tip the excess fat from the pan.

Stir 3 × 15ml spoons/3 tablespoons water into the pan, dislodging the sediment. Stir in 75g/3 oz butter, the shallots and the tarragon mustard. Cook over a high heat, whisking constantly with a wire whisk until the sauce begins to look slightly curdled. Stir in the remaining butter. Reduce the heat, add the mustard seeds and herbs and allow to simmer briefly.

Season the steaks with salt and pepper, cut them into slices, if liked and arrange the slices overlapping on 4 warmed plates. Spoon the sauce over. Or simply spoon the sauce over the whole steaks.

ESCALOPES OF CALVES LIVER WITH SMOOTH SHALLOT SAUCE

 15–20 minutes

25g/1 oz unsalted butter,
   diced
225g/8 oz shallots, finely
   chopped
450g/1 lb calves liver
50ml/2 fl oz Marsala
150ml/5 fl oz veal stock
50ml/2 fl oz whipping cream
1½–2 × 15ml spoons/
   1½–2 tablespoons chopped
   parsley
salt, freshly ground black
   pepper
lemon juice

FOR THE GARNISH

sprigs of parsley

Melt the butter, add the shallots, cover and cook over a low heat, shaking the pan occasionally for about 4 minutes until the shallots are soft.

Meanwhile, cut the liver into thin slices and grill for about 3 minutes each side so they remain pink in the centre.

Stir the Marsala into the softened shallots and boil rapidly until almost all the liquid has evaporated. Stir in the stock and cream and reduce by half. Purée well, then warm through gently in a clean pan.

Add the parsley and season with salt, pepper and lemon juice.

Spoon the sauce over 4 warmed plates. Place the liver on top and garnish with sprigs of parsley.

STEAK WITH BUTTERED SPRING ONIONS AND PARSLEY

  20 minutes

2 × 15ml spoons/
   2 tablespoons oil
75g/3 oz unsalted butter,
   diced
4 rump steaks, about 175g/
   6 oz each
salt, freshly ground black
   pepper
24 spring onions, cut down to
   leave 1.25cm/½ inch green
   part
1½ × 15ml spoons/
   1½ tablespoons finely
   chopped parsley
100ml/4 fl oz red vermouth
25ml/1 fl oz white vermouth
150ml/5 fl oz chicken stock
scant pinch French mustard

Heat the oil and 25g/1 oz butter in a frying pan. Add the steaks and cook for about 3 minutes each side.

Transfer the steaks to a warmed serving plate with tongs, season with salt and pepper and keep warm.

Meanwhile, put the spring onions, 25g/1 oz butter and 2 × 15ml spoons/2 tablespoons water into a medium frying pan and cook over a high heat, shaking the pan frequently. As the water evaporates, lower the heat and cook for 1–2 minutes until the onions soften slightly. Season and sprinkle the parsley over. Keep warm.

Tip the excess fat from the pan used for the steaks. Stir the red vermouth into the pan and boil until reduced to 3 × 15ml spoons/ 3 tablespoons.

Stir in the white vermouth and stock and reduce to 65ml/2½ fl oz.

Reduce the heat to very low and gradually swirl in the remaining butter, making sure each piece is incorporated before adding the next. Add the mustard and season to taste.

Place the steaks on warmed plates, spoon over the sauce and divide the spring onions and their cooking juices between the plates.

**STEAK WITH
BUTTERED SPRING ONIONS
AND PARSLEY**

79

BEEFBURGERS IN MUSHROOMS

 15–20 minutes

550g/1¼ lb rump steak,
  minced
2 × 15ml spoons/
  2 tablespoons beef marrow,
  finely chopped, if available
2 × 15ml spoons/
  2 tablespoons double cream
1 shallot, finely chopped
salt, freshly ground black
  pepper
50g/2 oz butter
15ml spoon/1 tablespoon oil
300ml/½ pint full-bodied red
  wine
1 shallot
8 oyster mushrooms or *large*
  flat mushrooms
200ml/7 fl oz brown veal stock
15ml spoon/1 tablespoon
  finely chopped parsley
10ml spoon/2 teaspoons finely
  chopped tarragon

FOR THE GARNISH

small sprigs of parsley

Mix together the steak, marrow, cream, chopped shallot, salt and pepper. Form into 4 burgers about 1.5cm/½ inch thick.

Heat half the butter with the oil in a heavy frying pan, add the burgers and cook over a high heat for about 2 minutes each side.

Meanwhile, boil the wine until it is reduced by three-quarters. Finely chop the shallot.

Transfer the burgers to a warm plate with tongs or a fish slice and keep warm.

Add a further 15g/½ oz butter to the pan, add the mushroom and shallot and cook for about 3 minutes over a moderate heat, turning the mushrooms over half-way through. Lift the mushrooms out with a perforated spoon and keep warm with the meat.

Stir the wine, then the stock into the pan and boil until reduced by half. Reduce the heat to very low and swirl in the remaining butter. Add the herbs, season, then spoon onto 4 warmed places.

Place 4 mushrooms in the sauce, then arrange the burgers and remaining mushrooms to resemble burgers in 'buns' of mushrooms. Garnish with sprigs of parsley.

NOISETTES OF LAMB
WITH HERB SAUCE

 20 minutes

65g/2½ oz unsalted butter,
  diced
4 noisettes of lamb, about
  2.5cm/1 inch thick
3 × 15ml spoons/
  3 tablespoons finely
  chopped shallot
1 clove of garlic, crushed
5ml spoon/1 teaspoon chopped
  thyme
5ml spoon/1 teaspoon finely
  chopped rosemary
5ml spoon/1 teaspoon finely
  chopped tarragon
5ml spoon/1 teaspoon finely
  chopped basil
225ml/8 fl oz medium-bodied
  dry white wine
2 × 15ml spoons/
  2 tablespoons crème fraîche
salt, freshly ground white
  pepper
flesh of 1 large tomato,
  coarsely chopped
10ml spoon/2 teaspoons finely
  chopped chives

Heat 25g/1 oz butter in a heavy-based frying pan, add the noisettes
and cook for about 3 minutes each side.

Transfer to a warmed plate with tongs and keep warm.

Add the shallot to the pan and cook for about 3 minutes, stirring
frequently, until softened.

Stir in the garlic and herbs and cook, stirring, for 30 seconds. Stir in
the wine and boil rapidly until reduced by half. Stir in the crème
fraîche and boil until slightly thickened.

Reduce the heat to very low and gradually whisk in the remaining
butter, making sure each piece is fully incorporated before adding the
next.

Season with salt and pepper and spoon onto 4 warmed plates.

Place the lamb on top and top each piece of lamb with tomato and
chives.

ITALIAN VEAL

PORK WITH PERNOD AND APRICOTS

 20 minutes

*6 ripe apricots, stoned and
    quartered*
*300ml/10 fl oz full-bodied dry
    white wine*
25g/1 oz unsalted butter
*4 escalopes of pork,
    100g/4 oz each*
50ml/2 fl oz double cream
*approx 15ml spoon/
    1 tablespoon Pernod*
*salt, freshly ground white
    pepper*
lemon juice

FOR THE GARNISH

sprigs of chervil

Put the apricots into a pan that they just fit in a single layer.

Add the wine, cover and poach the apricots gently for 4–5 minutes until just tender, turning them over if necessary to make sure that they cook evenly.

Meanwhile, heat half the butter in a large frying pan, add the pork and cook for 4–5 minutes, turning once.

Carefully lift the apricots from the wine with a perforated spoon. Place on a warmed plate and keep warm.

Remove the pork from the frying pan and keep warm.

Stir the poaching wine into the frying pan and boil rapidly until reduced to 50ml/2 fl oz. Stir in the cream and Pernod and boil briefly to thicken slightly.

Reduce the heat, swirl in the remaining butter and season with salt and white pepper. Add a little lemon juice, or a dash more Pernod according to taste.

Place the pork on 4 warmed plates, spoon the sauce over and place the apricot quarters in the sauce.

Garnish with sprigs of chervil.

ITALIAN VEAL

 20–25 minutes

*350ml/12 fl oz medium-bodied
    dry white wine*
*350ml/12 fl oz chicken or veal
    stock*
*40ml/1½ fl oz extra virgin
    olive oil*
*700g/1½ lb loin of veal, cut
    into thin slices and lightly
    pounded*
2 large shallots
10 good quality black olives
*50g/2 oz Italian sun-dried
    tomatoes in oil, rinsed,
    dried and cut into strips*
*10ml spoon/2 teaspoons finely
    chopped sage*
*15g/½ oz unsalted butter,
    diced*
squeeze of lemon juice
freshly ground black pepper

FOR THE GARNISH

sprigs of sage leaves

Boil the wine in a wide saucepan or frying pan until reduced by half. Add the stock and boil until reduced to 225ml/8 fl oz.

Meanwhile, heat the oil, add the veal and cook over a moderately high heat for about 2–3 minutes until lightly browned. Turn over with tongs or a fish slice, lower the heat to moderate and cook for about 2–3 minutes.

Meanwhile, finely chop the shallot and stone and chop the olives.

Transfer the veal to a warmed plate. Stir the shallots into the cooking juices and cook for about 10 seconds. Stir in the reduced liquid, dislodging any sediment, and bring to the boil.

Add the tomatoes and sage and boil until the liquid is reduced to 175ml/6 fl oz.

Stir in the olives. Reduce the heat and swirl in the butter.

Season with lemon juice and pepper.

Spoon the sauce over the veal and garnish with sage leaves.

VEAL BALLS WITH GOOSEBERRY SAUCE

 20–25 minutes

450g/1 lb lean veal, minced
50g/2 oz soft cheese
pinch of grated nutmeg
salt, freshly ground black
    pepper
1 egg white, beaten
6–8 × 15ml spoons/
    6–8 tablespoons toasted
    coriander seeds, crushed

FOR THE SAUCE

450g/1 lb gooseberries
25g/1 oz unsalted butter
salt, freshly ground black
    pepper
50g/2 oz sugar, to taste
lemon juice, optional

For the sauce, cook the gooseberries gently with the butter, a little salt and pepper and 50g/2 oz sugar in a covered saucepan until the juices run from the fruit.

Uncover the pan, increase the heat and cook to evaporate excess moisture.

Meanwhile, mix the veal, cheese, nutmeg, salt and pepper together thoroughly, then lightly mix in the egg white.

Gently form the mixture into 20 balls, then lightly press the coriander seeds into the surface of each.

Carefully lower the balls into a wide pan of just simmering water and cook for 3–4 minutes, turning them over gently half-way through.

When the gooseberries are cooked, process them briefly in a blender or food processor.

Reheat gently and adjust the seasoning and sweetness/sharpness. (Add a little lemon juice, if necessary.)

Remove the veal balls from the cooking liquor with a perforated spoon. If cooking them in batches, keep those that are ready warm in a warmed dish and cover with greaseproof paper.

Serve the sauce beside the balls on warmed plates.

CRISPY PORK IN APPLE BATTER

Serves 4–6

 20–25 minutes

100g/4 oz plain flour
salt
2.5ml/½ teaspoon ground
    cinnamon
150ml/¼ pint thick apple
    purée (made from 1 large
    cooking apple)
4 × 15ml spoons/
    4 tablespoons cider
1 egg white
450g/1 lb fillet of pork, cut
    into 1.5–2cm/½–¾ inch
    pieces
freshly ground white pepper
oil for deep-frying
mint hollandaise (see page
    121) to serve, optional

Mix the flour, salt and cinnamon together in a bowl.

Blend together the apple purée and cider, pour onto the dry ingredients, then gradually stir the dry ingredients into the apple to make a smooth batter. Whisk the egg white, then fold it lightly into the batter.

Season the pieces of pork with salt and pepper then divide into 2 or 3 batches according to the size of pan you will be using for cooking them–it is important that they should not be crowded. Coat one batch lightly in batter.

Cook these pieces in deep hot oil, at 180°C/350°F for about 4 minutes, turning them over half-way through.

Meanwhile, coat another batch of pork in batter. Drain the cooked cubes on absorbent paper and keep warm while coating and cooking the remaining pieces. Check the oil temperature between batches.

If the first batch of pork has lost its crispness by the time the last is cooked, pop it briefly back into the hot oil.

Serve with mint hollandaise, if liked.

FILLET OF LAMB BAKED IN SALT WITH HERBS

15 minutes cooking, then 5–10 minutes resting

2 fillets of young lamb, about 400g/14 oz each
large piece of fat from the saddle
10 small sprigs rosemary
10 small sprigs sage
10 small sprigs lemon thyme
salt, freshly ground black pepper
200g/7 oz plain flour
175g/6 oz sea salt
100ml/4 fl oz dry white wine

In a roasting tin, place a layer of the back fat to fit under the fillets. Place 2 sprigs of each herb in the fat and season with black pepper, then place the fillets on the herbs. Cover with the remaining herbs and sprinkle again with black pepper.

Mix the flour, sea salt and wine together. Spread the mixture with your fingers over and down the sides of each fillet.

Roast in a hot oven, 220°C/425°F/Gas 7, for 12–15 minutes.

Transfer the meat to a wire rack and leave for 5–10 minutes, then remove the crusts and herbs and cut the lamb into slices.

VEAL WITH LIGHT LETTUCE SOUFFLÉ STUFFING

15 minutes + 15 minutes cooking

15ml spoon/1 tablespoon medium-bodied dry white wine
15ml spoon/1 tablespoon finely chopped white part of leek
75g/3 oz lettuce
4 veal escalopes, about 150g/5 oz each
salt, freshly ground white pepper
squeeze of lemon juice
75g/3 oz Ricotta cheese
1 egg white

Heat the wine in a saucepan, add the leeks, cover and cook for 2–3 minutes, shaking the pan occasionally.

Meanwhile, finely shred the lettuce, add to the pan, cover again and cook until the lettuce has fallen. Uncover the pan and drive off excess moisture, if necessary.

Meanwhile, beat the escalopes to flatten them and season with salt, pepper and lemon juice. Place on a buttered baking tray.

Purée the lettuce and leek with the Ricotta – the mixture does not have to be completely smooth. Whisk the egg white until stiff but not dry, then fold in the purée with salt and pepper to taste.

Place some of the mixture onto half of each escalope, then fold the other half lightly over the stuffing.

Cook in a moderately hot oven, 190°C/375°F/Gas 5, for about 15 minutes until the stuffing is just set.

Leave for about a minute before carefully removing from the tray with a fish slice.

VEAL WITH CUCUMBER AND MANGETOUT PEAS

 25 minutes

2 × 15ml spoons/
  2 tablespoons olive oil
25g/1 oz unsalted butter
700g/1½ lb fillet of veal, cut
  into 3cm/1¼ inch cubes
50g/2 oz spring onions,
  chopped
300ml/10 fl oz medium-bodied
  dry white wine
1 cucumber
175ml/6 fl oz chicken or veal
  stock
225g/8 oz mangetout peas
90ml/6 tablespoons soured
  cream

FOR THE GARNISH

2 × 15ml spoons/
  2 tablespoons chopped
  chives

Heat the oil and butter in a large frying pan, add the veal, and cook, stirring frequently, for 2–3 minutes. Remove with a perforated spoon and keep warm.

Add the spring onions to the pan and cook for a minute, stirring occasionally. Stir in the wine and boil hard until reduced by half.

Meanwhile, peel the cucumber, remove the seeds and cut into 2cm/¾ inch dice.

Stir the stock into the reduced wine, bring to the boil, add the mangetout peas and cucumber, cover and simmer for about 5 minutes, or until just crisp.

Stir in the soured cream, boil briefly until slightly thickened, then return the veal to the pan.

Check the seasoning and sprinkle chives over.

SLICED PORK IN SPICED MILK

 10 minutes + 30–35 minutes

4 slices boned and rolled loin
  of pork, well trimmed
1 lemon
15g/½ oz unsalted butter
425ml/¾ pint milk
5ml spoon/1 teaspoon
  coriander seeds, lightly
  toasted
5ml/spoon/1 teaspoon
  cardamom seeds
4 small cloves
long strip of tangerine,
  mandarin, clementine or
  orange rind
salt, freshly ground black
  pepper

FOR THE GARNISH

sprigs of fresh coriander

Rub the pork all over with lemon.

Heat the butter in a frying pan or shallow flame-proof dish that the pork will fit in a single layer, add the pork and cook for about 1½ minutes each side until 'set' on the surface.

Meanwhile, pound the coriander and cardamom together. Pour the milk into the pan or dish, add the spices, tangerine rind, salt and pepper and bring to simmering point. Adjust the heat so the liquid just moves, cover and cook for about 30–35 minutes until the pork is tender.

Transfer the meat to a warmed plate and boil the liquid, if necessary, until reduced to 200ml/7 fl oz.

Place the meat on 4 warmed plates. Strain the liquor over and garnish with coriander.

VEAL WITH CUCUMBER
AND MANGETOUT PEAS

'BOILED' BEEF WITH CARROTS, PARSLEY DUMPLINGS AND GRAVY

 30 minutes

1.1 litres/2 pints brown veal stock
sprig of parsley
sprig of thyme
2 sage leaves
2 bay leaves
4 tournedos, about 150g/5 oz each
350g/12 oz small new carrots, tops left on, or slightly larger carrots cut into 5mm/⅛ inch slices
200ml/7 fl oz medium-bodied red wine

FOR THE DUMPLINGS

50g/2 oz self-raising flour
salt and freshly ground black pepper
15ml spoon/1 tablespoon chopped parsley
15g/½ oz butter, finely diced
approx 1 egg, beaten

TO DECORATE

flat-leaved parsley, optional

Boil the stock in a wide saucepan with the herbs until reduced by half.

Meanwhile, to make the dumplings, mix the flour with the salt, pepper and parsley, stir in the butter, then add the egg and mix until smooth.

Drop small teaspoonfuls of the mixture into a wide pan of simmering salted water. Cover and cook for 10 minutes, turning half-way through.

Meanwhile, lower the steaks into the stock, adjust the heat so the liquid just simmers and cook for 5–8 minutes so they are rare.

Steam the carrots, 6–7 minutes for whole new baby ones, 4–5 minutes for sliced old ones, until just tender.

Boil the wine in a wide pan until reduced to 25ml/1 fl oz.

Lift the beef from the stock with a perforated spoon and place on 4 warmed plates. Stir 225ml/7 fl oz of the poaching liquid into the reduced wine, spoon a little onto the plates and arrange the carrots and dumplings on top.

'BOILED' BEEF WITH CARROTS,
PARSLEY DUMPLINGS
AND GRAVY

MINI RACKS OF LAMB WITH CREAMY HAM AND MUSHROOM STUFFING

 25 minutes + 11 minutes cooking

8 lamb cutlets about 2cm/¾ inch thick
50ml/2 fl oz medium-bodied dry white wine
100ml/4 fl oz sercial madeira
300ml/10 fl oz veal stock
40g/1½ oz unsalted butter, diced

FOR THE GARNISH

sprigs of parsley

FOR THE STUFFING

15g/½ oz unsalted butter
1 shallot, finely chopped
100g/4 oz button mushrooms, finely chopped
100g/4 oz ham, finely chopped
25g/1 oz soft cheese
2.5ml spoon/½ teaspoon finely chopped thyme
6 × 15ml spoons/ 6 tablespoons fresh breadcrumbs
1 small egg, beaten
salt, freshly ground black pepper

For the stuffing, heat the butter, add the shallot and cook for 2 minutes. Stir in the mushrooms and cook for 3 minutes, stirring frequently. Stir in the ham, cheese and thyme.

Remove from the heat and stir in the breadcrumbs, egg, salt and pepper. Continue to stir for a minute or two to cool the mixture slightly.

Carefully spread the mixture on one side of 4 of the cutlets. Place another cutlet on top, then stand the pairs upright on their flat ends. Secure them with string, then stand in a roasting tin and cook in a hot oven, 220°C/425°F/Gas 7 for 8 minutes. Reduce the heat to moderately hot 190°C/375°F/Gas 5, and cook for about another 3 minutes. They should be pink inside.

Transfer the cutlets to a warmed plate, cover and keep warm.

Pour any excess fat from the roasting tin, then stir the wine and madeira into the cooking juices and boil rapidly until reduced to about 25ml/1 fl oz. Stir in the stock and reduce to about 175ml/6 fl oz. Lower the heat and gradually stir in the butter, making sure each piece is fully incorporated before adding the next. Season to taste.

Remove the strings from the cutlets, spoon the sauce onto 4 warmed plates, and stand the cutlets on top. Garnish with sprigs of parsley.

BEEF WITH LOVAGE

 15 minutes + 25–30 minutes cooking

4 rump steaks
4 sprigs lovage
salt, freshly ground black
pepper
15ml/spoon/1 tablespoon oil
25g/1 oz mustard and cress
1 small carrot, finely chopped
2 sticks celery, finely chopped
1 shallot, finely chopped
15ml spoon/1 tablespoon
finely chopped lovage
4 × 15ml spoons/
4 tablespoons red wine
2.5ml spoon/½ teaspoon
tomato purée

With the point of a small sharp knife, cut a pocket through one side of each steak. Put a sprig of lovage in each pocket. Season the outsides of the steak with salt and pepper.

Heat the oil in a frying pan over a moderately high heat and cook the steaks for about 1½ minutes on each side to seal the surface.

Meanwhile, divide the vegetables and chopped lovage between 4 large pieces of foil. Place the steaks on top and fold the sides of the foil up.

Pour the wine over the steaks, then fold the foil over to form a loose parcel. Seal the edges well.

Place the parcels in a moderate oven, 180°C/350°F/Gas 4 for about 25–30 minutes, depending on the thickness of the steaks (the vegetables will be crisp).

Tip the juices from the parcels into a frying pan, stir in the tomato purée and boil until slightly thickened. Season to taste.

Place the steaks and vegetables on 4 warmed plates and spoon the sauce over.

PORK WITH GRAPES AND CHESTNUTS

 20 minutes + 35 minutes cooking

25g/1 oz unsalted butter
3 × 15ml spoons/
3 tablespoons finely
chopped shallots
550g/1¼ lb boned loin of pork,
cut into 2.5cm/1 inch cubes
175ml/6 fl oz chicken stock
100ml/4 fl oz ginger wine
sprig of thyme
salt, freshly ground black
pepper
squeeze of lemon juice
16 chestnuts canned in brine,
drained
100g/4 oz seedless green
grapes

Heat the butter in an ovenproof casserole, add the shallots and cook over a moderately low heat for about 3 minutes, stirring frequently.

Stir in the pork and cook for a further 3–4 minutes, stirring occasionally. Stir in the stock and ginger wine and bring just to the boil.

Add the thyme, salt, pepper and juice, cover tightly and cook over a low heat, so that the liquid just moves, for 25 minutes.

Add the chestnuts, cover again and cook for 5 minutes. Add the grapes, cover again and cook for a further 5 minutes.

Transfer the meat, chestnuts and grapes with a perforated spoon to a warmed plate.

Boil the cooking liquor until reduced to 100ml/4 fl oz. Remove the thyme and adjust the seasoning. Spoon onto 4 warmed plates.
Arrange the pork, chestnuts and grapes on the sauce.

LAMB WITH
OLIVES AND LEMON

LAMB WITH OLIVES AND LEMON

 20 minutes + 30 minutes cooking

2 × 15ml spoons/2
   tablespoons olive oil
2 shallots, finely chopped
700g/1½ lb boneless loin of
   lamb, cut into 2.5 cm/1 inch
   cubes
100ml/4 fl oz full-bodied dry
   white wine
75ml/3 fl oz dry vermouth
5ml spoon/1 teaspoon finely
   grated lemon rind
4 × 15ml spoons/
   4 tablespoons lemon juice
175g/6 oz green olives
2–3 × 5ml spoons/
   2–3 teaspoons chopped
   tarragon
salt, freshly ground black
   pepper
15g/½ oz unsalted butter

FOR THE GARNISH

segments of lemon, peel and
   pith removed

Heat the oil in a flameproof casserole, add the shallots and lamb and cook, stirring occasionally, until the lamb has just softened.

Stir in the wine, vermouth, lemon rind and juice and bring to just below boiling point. Reduce the heat to very low, cover tightly and cook for 20 minutes.

Stone the olives. Add the olives, tarragon, salt and pepper. Cover again and cook for a further 10 minutes.

Strain the liquid into a frying pan and boil until reduced to about 100ml/4 fl oz. Reduce the heat to very low and swirl in the butter. Adjust the seasoning. Pass through a sieve, if liked, then reheat gently.

Spoon the sauce onto 4 warmed plates. Arrange the lamb and olives on the plates and garnish with lemon.

GAME

Breast of pheasant with pine nut sauce
Venison with redcurrant sauce and cranberries
Venison with port sauce and mangetout peas
Medallions of hare with blueberries
Pheasant breasts with white wine and orange

BREAST OF PHEASANT WITH PINE NUT SAUCE

 15 minutes

25g/1 oz unsalted butter
4 pheasant breasts
3 shallots, finely chopped
200ml/7 fl oz medium-bodied dry white wine
50g/2 oz pine nuts
150ml/¼ pint crème fraîche
pinch of ground coriander
pinch of ground mace
5ml spoon/1 teaspoon lime juice
salt, freshly ground black pepper

FOR THE GARNISH

short, fine strips of lime, blanched

Heat half the butter in a non-stick frying pan, add the pheasant breasts, skin-side down, and cook for 3 minutes. Turn them over with tongs and cook for a further 2–3 minutes, so they remain pink.

Meanwhile, heat the remaining butter in another frying pan, preferably non-stick, add the shallots and 25ml/1 fl oz wine, cover and cook over a moderately low heat, shaking the pan occasionally, for 3–4 minutes. Add the remaining wine and the nuts and boil until the liquid is reduced to 50ml/2 fl oz.

When the pheasant breasts are cooked, transfer them to a warmed plate with tongs, cover and keep warm.

Stir the crème fraîche, coriander and mace into the reduced wine and boil for a few minutes until slightly thickened. Add the lime juice, salt and pepper.

Remove the skin from the breasts and either cut the breasts into thin slices, or leave them whole.

Spoon the sauce over 4 warmed plates and arrange the breasts on top. Scatter short, fine strips of lime peel over.

VENISON WITH REDCURRANT SAUCE AND CRANBERRIES

 15 minutes

12 mignons of venison, about 40g/1½ oz each
225ml/8 fl oz full-bodied red wine
50ml/2 fl oz ruby port
300ml/10 fl oz game stock
small sprig of rosemary
100g/4 oz cranberries
75g/3 oz caster sugar
approx 15ml spoon/ 1 tablespoon redcurrant jelly
25g/1 oz unsalted butter, diced
salt, freshly ground black pepper

FOR THE GARNISH

sprigs of thyme

Grill the venison under a high heat for 1 minute each side.

Meanwhile, boil the wine in a frying pan until it is reduced to 2 × 15ml spoons/2 tablespoons. Transfer the venison to a warmed plate with tongs, cover and keep warm

Stir the port into the wine, reduce slightly, then stir in the stock and rosemary and reduce by half.

Meanwhile simmer the cranberries for 3 minutes. Remove from the heat, stir in sugar to taste, strain and keep warm.

Stir the redcurrant jelly into the sauce and boil to reduce slightly. Remove the rosemary. Gradually swirl in the butter, making sure each piece is incorporated before adding the next.

Spoon the sauce onto 4 warmed plates. Place the venison on top, arrange the cranberries around and garnish with sprigs of thyme.

VENISON WITH PORT SAUCE AND MANGETOUT PEAS

 15 minutes

300ml/½ pint veal stock
salt, freshly ground black
   pepper
12 mignons of venison, about
   40g/1½ oz each
15ml/1 tablespoon raspberry
   vinegar
100ml/4 fl oz medium-bodied
   red wine
100ml/4 fl oz ruby port
100g/4 oz mangetout peas,
   thinly sliced
40g/1½ oz unsalted butter,
   diced

Boil the stock in a frying pan until reduced to 75ml/3 fl oz.

Meanwhile, season the venison and grill for 1 minute each side, then keep warm.

Stir the vinegar, wine and port into the reduced stock and boil down to 150ml/5 fl oz.

Blanch the mangetout peas in boiling salted water for 45 seconds. Drain well.

Gradually stir the butter into the sauce over a low heat, making sure each piece is fully incorporated before adding the next. Season with salt and pepper.

Spoon the sauce onto 4 warmed plates, place the venison on top and place some slices of mangetout on each mignon.

MEDALLIONS OF HARE WITH BLUEBERRIES

 15 minutes

25g/1 oz unsalted butter
12 medallions of young hare,
   about 50g/2 oz each
3 × 15ml spoons/
   3 tablespoons eau-de-vie de
   myrtilles or framboise
100ml/4 fl oz sweetish white
   vermouth
100g/4 oz blueberries
3 × 15ml spoons/
   3 tablespoons crème fraîche
   or double cream
salt, freshly ground black
   pepper
lemon juice

Heat the butter in a heavy frying pan, add the medallions and cook for 1½–2 minutes each side. Transfer the hare to a warmed plate with tongs, cover and keep warm.

Stir the eau-de-vie into the pan, bring to the boil then stir in the vermouth and reduce by half.

Meanwhile, in a separate pan, simmer the blueberries and crème fraîche or cream until slightly reduced. Stir into the frying pan, boil if necessary to adjust the consistency, then season with salt, pepper and lemon juice.

Spoon the sauce onto 4 warmed plates and arrange the medallions on it.

VENISON WITH PORT SAUCE
AND MANGETOUT PEAS

PHEASANT BREASTS WITH WHITE WINE AND ORANGE

 20 minutes

75g/3 oz unsalted butter,
   diced
4 pheasant breasts
175ml/5 fl oz fruity
   medium-bodied dry white
   wine, eg Alsatian muscat
100ml/4 fl oz dry vermouth
225ml/8 fl oz veal stock
3 sprigs chervil, optional
4 black peppercorns, lightly
   crushed
200ml/7 fl oz orange juice
salt

FOR THE GARNISH

sprigs of chervil

Heat half of the butter in a frying pan, add the breasts skin-side down in a single layer and cook for 3 minutes. Turn the breasts over with tongs and cook for a further 3 minutes.

Meanwhile, boil the wine and vermouth until reduced to about 25ml/1 fl oz, then stir in the stock, add the chervil and peppercorns and boil until reduced to 150ml/5 fl oz.

Transfer the breasts to a warmed plate with tongs, cover and keep warm.

Stir the orange juice into the frying pan and boil rapidly until reduced to 50ml/2 fl oz. Stir in the reduced stock and bring to the boil.

Remove the peppercorns and chervil with a perforated spoon (or pass through a sieve if you want a really clear, smooth sauce, then reheat in a clean pan). Over a low heat gradually swirl in the remaining butter. Season to taste.

Remove the skin from the breasts, cut the breasts into slices, if you like, then re-form and keep warm.

Spoon the sauce onto 4 warmed plates and place the breasts on the sauce arranged in a fan shape. Garnish with sprigs of chervil.

VEGETABLES

Steamed parsley
Courgettes with lemon and chervil
Lettuce with grapes
Artichokes with oregano
Ratatouille with fennel

STEAMED PARSLEY

 5 minutes

75g/3 oz parsley, stems
   removed
4 × 15ml spoons/
   4 tablespoons butter
10ml spoon/2 teaspoons lemon
   juice
salt, freshly ground black
   pepper

Steam the parsley for 50–60 seconds, then remove immediately from the heat.

   Melt the butter with the lemon juice, salt and pepper.

   Toss the parsley with 2 forks, pour the butter over and toss lightly. Serve immediately.

COURGETTES WITH LEMON AND CHERVIL

  8–10 minutes

350g/12 oz slim courgettes,
   thinly sliced
salt
long strip of lemon rind
15 sprigs of chervil
2 × 15ml spoons/
   2 tablespoons lemon juice

FOR THE GARNISH

chopped chervil

Steam the courgettes over salted water containing the lemon rind and sprigs of chervil for 3 minutes.

   Warm the lemon juice in a small saucepan.

   Transfer the courgettes to a warmed dish, sprinkle with lemon juice, then garnish with chopped chervil.

LETTUCE WITH GRAPES

  10 minutes + 10 minutes cooking

4 tight-hearted round lettuces,
   cut into quarters
salt, freshly ground black
   pepper
75g/3 oz seedless white grapes
75ml/3 fl oz dry white wine
75ml/3 fl oz chicken stock or
   water
40g/1½ oz unsalted butter,
   diced

Cook the lettuce in boiling salted water for 1 minute, then turn into a colander and put under cold running water. Drain well and gently press out excess moisture.

   Pack the lettuce quarters into a heavy frying pan or shallow flameproof casserole that they will just fit in a single layer. Pack the grapes in amongst the lettuce, then pour in the wine and stock. Bring to simmering point, cover tightly and cook gently for about 10 minutes until the lettuce is tender.

   Transfer the lettuce and grapes to a warmed serving dish with a perforated spoon.

   Boil the cooking liquor rapidly until syrupy.

   Reduce the heat to very low and gradually whisk in the butter, making sure each piece is incorporated before adding the next.

   Pour over the lettuce and grapes.

COURGETTES WITH LEMON
AND CHERVIL

101

ARTICHOKES WITH OREGANO

 20–25 minutes

4 artichokes
salt, freshly ground black
     pepper
lemon juice
3 shallots, finely chopped
2 × 15ml spoons/
     2 tablespoons olive oil
175ml/6 fl oz chicken stock
1½ × 15ml spoons/
     1½ tablespoons lemon juice
5ml spoon/1 teaspoon chopped
     oregano
inside leaves of 2 round
     lettuces
2 × 15ml spoons/
     2 tablespoons finely
     chopped parsley
1 punnet of mustard and cress

Cut the artichokes into quarters, cut away the hairy chokes, then put the artichokes immediately into simmering salted water acidulated with lemon juice for 15–20 minutes until tender.

Meanwhile, cook the shallots in the oil, stirring occasionally until softened, but do not allow to colour. Stir in the stock, lemon juice and oregano and boil until reduced to 75ml/3 fl oz.

Arrange the lettuce leaves to form small 'nests' on 4 plates and divide half the parsley and the mustard and cress between the 'nests'.

Drain the artichokes. Remove the leaves, cut each base in half, then stir into the sauce with the remaining parsley. Check the seasoning then divide between the 'nests'.

RATATOUILLE WITH FENNEL

  30 minutes

2 × 15ml spoons/
     2 tablespoons olive oil
2 × 15ml spoons/
     2 tablespoons walnut or
     hazelnut oil
150g/5 oz onions, thinly sliced
150g/5 oz fennel bulb, thinly
     sliced
2 cloves garlic
salt, freshly ground black
     pepper
2 medium sized red peppers
1 small green pepper
1 small aubergine, about
     175g/6 oz
450g/1 lb large tomatoes
175g/6 oz slim courgettes

FOR THE GARNISH

finely chopped herbs

Heat half of each oil in a large frying pan, add the onions and fennel and cook over a low heat.

Crush the garlic to a paste with a pinch of salt, add to the pan and cook over a moderate heat, stirring occasionally, for 5 minutes.

Meanwhile, slice the peppers and aubergine. Add the remaining oil to the pan and stir in the peppers and aubergine. Cook, stirring occasionally, for 10 minutes.

Meanwhile, skin and remove the seeds from the tomatoes, then roughly chop the flesh. Slice the courgettes.

Stir the tomato flesh and courgettes into the pan and cook for 10 minutes, stirring occasionally. Season with salt and pepper.

Serve sprinkled with plenty of chopped herbs, as a vegetable accompaniment to a main course, or as a light course with bread and perhaps cheese or pâté.

DESSERTS

Mango compote
Flaming ice cream
White peaches with raspberry purée
Fruit fondue
Strawberry pastries
Sautéed bananas
Berry and tropical fruit salad
Maple walnut sabayon
Grilled pears with caramel sauce
Fruit salad of lychees, raspberries and melon
Baked stuffed figs
Apples and pears with Drambuie cream
Pistachio 'petits pots'
Chocolate mousse
Lemon soufflés
Wine-poached rhubarb

FLAMING ICE CREAM

MANGO COMPOTE

 5 minutes

3 large ripe mangoes, chilled,
    peeled, stoned and cut into
    slices
about 7.5ml spoon/1½
    teaspoons lime juice
about 150ml/5 fl oz good
    quality dessert wine, chilled

TO DECORATE

small strips of lemon balm or
    lemon thyme

Lay the slices of mango in 4 cold serving bowls. Sprinkle with lime
juice and pour the wine over. Cover and chill while the rest of the meal
is being eaten or for 1–1¼ hours.
    Serve decorated with small sprigs of lemon balm or lemon thyme.

FLAMING ICE CREAM

 10 minutes

75g/3 oz plain chocolate,
    chopped
50ml/2 fl oz double cream
2½ × 15ml spoons/
    2½ tablespoons cognac
2½ × 15ml spoons/
    2½ tablespoons coffee
    liqueur
600ml/1 pint vanilla ice cream
50g/2 oz flaked almonds,
    toasted

Gently heat the chocolate and cream together in a small heavy
saucepan, stirring with a wooden spoon, until the chocolate has
melted. Do not allow it to become too hot.
    Warm the cognac and the coffee liqueur.
    Scoop the ice cream into 4 dishes or onto 4 plates.
    Spoon the chocolate sauce over and scatter with almonds.
    Light the cognac and liqueur with a taper, then pour, while still
flaming, over the desserts.

WHITE PEACHES WITH
RASPBERRY PURÉE

 10 minutes

4 ripe peaches
approx 5ml spoon/1 teaspoon
    kirsch
approx 5ml spoon/1 teaspoon
    Cointreau
275g/10 oz raspberries
40g/1½ oz icing sugar, to taste
lemon juice, to taste

TO DECORATE

mint leaves

Peel the peaches, cut them in half, discarding the stones.
    Mix the kirsch and Cointreau together, then sprinkle over the peach
slices.
    Purée the raspberries in a blender then pass through a nylon sieve.
Sweeten to taste with sugar and add a little lemon juice to 'lift' the
flavour.
    Spoon the purée over 4 cold plates, then arrange the peach slices on
top. Decorate with mint leaves.

FRUIT FONDUE

  10 minutes

10ml spoon/2 teaspoons
   cornflour
1 egg yolk
300ml/½ pint orange juice
finely grated rind of 1 orange
15ml spoon/1 tablespoon
   lemon juice
finely grated rind of 1 large
   lemon
4 × 15ml spoons/
   4 tablespoons melted
   unsalted butter
3 × 15ml spoons/
   3 tablespoons Mandarin
   Napoleon, or other orange
   liqueur
approx 100g/4 oz caster sugar
prepared fruits, such as
   pineapple cubes, seedless
   grapes, orange segments,
   pieces of pear or apple
   dipped in lime or lemon
   juice, pieces of peach,
   nectarine, mango or
   papaya, strawberries
marshmallows, firm chocolate
   truffles, chocolate coated
   biscuits or cubes of cake,
   for dipping

Blend the cornflour and egg yolk with a little of the orange juice.

Bring the remaining orange juice to the boil, then stir into the cornflour mixture. Return this to the saucepan and cook over a moderately low heat until thickened, stirring constantly.

Blend together the orange rind and lemon juice and rind, butter and liqueur, then stir into the sauce and warm through. Serve either in a pottery fondue pot, a single bowl or individual bowls over small burners.

Arrange the dips of sugar, fruit, marshmallows etc. attractively around.

STRAWBERRY PASTRIES

 10 minutes + 5 minutes cooking

8 squares filo pastry, approx
   6.5cm/2½ inches square
melted unsalted butter
beaten egg
4 medium-large round
   strawberrries

TO SERVE

fromage blanc or thick plain
   yoghurt, decorated with
   mint leaves

Place 4 of the filo squares on a non-stick or greased baking sheet, then brush with melted butter. Place another square on top, brush with melted butter and brush around the edges with beaten egg. Stand a strawberry in the centre of each square, then fold the pastry up around it, twisting the corners together over the strawberry.

Bake in a hot oven, 220°C/425°F/Gas 7, for about 5 minutes, until the pastry is light golden and crisp.

Serve with the decorated fromage blanc or thick plain yoghurt.

FRUIT FONDUE

SAUTÉED BANANAS

  10 minutes

40g/1½ oz unsalted butter,
  diced
4 firm bananas, split
  lengthways
40g/1½ oz soft brown sugar
15ml spoon/1 tablespoon
  lemon juice
3 × 15ml spoons/
  3 tablespoons orange juice
10ml/spoon/2 teaspoons
  orange rind
4 × 5ml spoons/4 teaspoons
  dark rum
4 × 5ml spoons/4 teaspoons
  orange liqueur or
  Benedictine

TO SERVE

wedges of lemon

Heat the butter in a frying pan, add the bananas and cook them
lightly and quickly over a high heat, turning them over carefully.
Remove carefully with a perforated spoon and keep warm.

Stir the sugar, fruit juices and orange rind into the pan and boil
until just syrupy, but not caramelized. Stir in the rum and orange
liqueur or Benedictine and set alight with a lighted taper.

When the flames have subsided, return the bananas to the pan and
heat through briefly.

Serve accompanied by wedges of lemon.

BERRY AND TROPICAL
FRUIT SALAD

 10 minutes

2 passionfruits
15ml spoon/1 tablespoon lime
  juice
5ml spoon/1 teaspoon lime
  rind
few drops Angostura bitters
15ml spoon/1 tablespoon icing
  sugar, to taste
1 mango, peeled and sliced
100g/4 oz blueberries or
  blackberries
100g/4 oz raspberries
100g/4 oz loganberries
5 sprigs of mint

Cut the passionfruits in half. Scoop out the seeds and flesh with a
teaspoon into a sieve. Press the flesh through. Discard the seeds.

Combine the flesh with the lime juice and rind, Angostura bitters
and sugar to taste.

Place the mango, blueberries or blackberries, raspberries and
loganberries in a cold bowl. Shred some of the mint leaves and add to
the bowl. Spoon the sauce over and toss lightly.

Divide the salad between 4 cold plates. Spoon any remaining sauce
over and decorate with the remaining mint.

MAPLE WALNUT SABAYON

 15 minutes

4 egg yolks
50ml/2 fl oz maple syrup
90ml/3½ fl oz medium-bodied
    dry white wine
40g/1½ oz chopped walnuts

TO SERVE

tuiles d'amande

Whisk the egg yolks, maple syrup and wine together in a bowl placed over a saucepan of simmering water until thick and very frothy.

Meanwhile, spread the nuts out on a baking sheet and toast lightly under a hot grill, stirring frequently to ensure they brown evenly.

Pour the sabayon into 4 custard cups or warmed glasses and sprinkle the nuts over.

Serve immediately with tuiles d'amande.

GRILLED PEARS WITH CARAMEL SAUCE

 15 minutes

4 ripe pears
lemon juice
25g/1 oz unsalted butter,
    melted
sugar, for sprinkling
75g/3 oz sugar
175ml/6 fl oz double cream
few drops of vanilla flavouring
5 ml spoon/1 teaspoon cold
    unsalted butter

Peel the pears, cut in halves lengthways and remove the cores. Brush the cut surfaces with lemon juice. With the point of a sharp knife, score the surface of the pears.

Place the pears, cut side down, on a grill rack covered with buttered foil, brush them with melted butter and sprinkle sugar over. Place under the grill for about 5 minutes until golden brown.

Meanwhile, gently heat the 75g/3 oz sugar, stirring with a wooden spoon, until it dissolves, then heat until golden brown. Remove from the heat immediately and stir in 3 × 15ml spoons/3 tablespoons hot water – be careful as the mixture may spatter. Stir in the cream, making sure all the caramel has dissolved, then bring to the boil over a moderate heat and boil briefly to thicken slightly.

Remove the caramel sauce from the heat, stir in the vanilla flavouring and swirl in the cold butter.

Spoon some of the sauce over 4 warmed plates and place the pear halves on the sauce. Serve the remaining sauce separately in a warmed jug.

FRUIT SALAD OF LYCHEES, RASPBERRIES AND MELON

 15 minutes

4 ratafias, crushed
4 × 5ml spoons/4 teaspoons
  eau-de-vie de framboise
1 small Ogen melon
8 lychees, peeled, stoned and
  halved or quartered,
  depending on size
100g/4 oz raspberries
approx 300ml/½ pint good
  quality sparkling dry white
  wine.

FOR THE GARNISH

sprigs of mint

Put the ratafias in the bottom of 4 large cold champagne flutes or similar tall glasses. Sprinkle with eau-de-vie.

Halve the melon, discard the seeds and scoop the flesh into balls with a melon baller, or cut it into cubes with a sharp knife.

Divide the fruit between the glasses, putting them in alternately.

Pour sparkling wine over immediately before serving and garnish with sprigs of mint.

Note: The fruit, wine and glasses should be chilled beforehand, if possible.

BAKED STUFFED FIGS

  10 minutes + 10 minutes cooking

8 large black figs
90g/3½ oz soft cheese
3 × 15ml spoons/
  3 tablespoons finely
  chopped preserved ginger
3 × 15ml spoons/
  3 tablespoons caster sugar
3 × 15ml spoons/
  3 tablespoons syrup from
  the jar of ginger
2 × 15ml spoons/2
  tablespoons finely grated
  orange rind

TO SERVE

whipped cream or crème
  fraîche

Cut the top quarter or third from the figs, then make a deep indentation in each bottom section.

Beat the cheese to soften it, then mix in the ginger and sugar. Press this mixture into the indentations and cover with the tops.

Blend 3 × 15ml spoons/3 tablespoons water into the ginger syrup.

Place the figs in a shallow ovenproof dish, spoon the syrup over and cook in a moderate oven, 180°C/350°F/Gas 4, for 10 minutes, basting half-way through with the juices.

Carefully transfer to 4 warmed plates. Mix the orange rind with the juices and spoon over the figs.

Serve with whipped cream or crème fraîche, if liked.

FRUIT SALAD OF LYCHEES,
RASPBERRIES AND MELON

APPLES AND PEARS WITH DRAMBUIE CREAM

 20 minutes

50–75g/2–3 oz sugar
300ml/½ pint fruity dry white
   wine, eg Alsatian muscat
350g/12 oz Bramley's apples,
   peeled, cored and sliced
2 Comice pears, peeled, cored
   and sliced
seeds from 4 green cardamom
   pods
225ml/8 fl oz whipping cream
approx 2 × 15ml spoons/
   2 tablespoons Drambuie, to
   taste

Dissolve the sugar in the wine in a large frying pan over a low heat, stirring frequently.

Lay the slices of apples and pears in the wine syrup, sprinkle the cardamom seeds over, cover and poach the fruit gently for about 10 minutes until just tender.

Meanwhile whip the cream with the Drambuie.

Remove the fruit with a perforated spoon. Boil the juices rapidly until reduced by half.

Arrange the fruit on 4 plates or 1 large one. Spoon the juices over the fruit and serve with the cream.

PISTACHIO 'PETITS POTS'

 10 minutes + 20–25 minutes cooking

60g/2½ oz caster sugar
300ml/½ pint double cream
100g/4 oz pistachio nuts,
   ground
3 egg yolks

TO DECORATE

wild strawberries, or sliced
   strawberries
chopped pistachios

Heat the sugar with the cream in a heavy-based saucepan, stirring with a wooden spoon until the sugar has dissolved.

Stir in the nuts and bring to the boil. Remove from the heat and remove any skin from the surface.

Beat the egg yolks.

Place 4 individual buttered heatproof dishes in a baking tin.

Stir the cream into the eggs and pour into the dishes. Surround the dishes with boiling water, cover them with greaseproof paper and cook in a moderately low oven, 170°C/325°F/Gas 3, for about 20–25 minutes until just set.

Remove from the heat and allow to cool slightly before unmoulding.

Surround with wild strawberries or sliced strawberries. Scatter chopped pistachios on top of the 'petits pots'.

PISTACHIO 'PETIT POTS'

CHOCOLATE MOUSSE

 10 minutes + 15 minutes standing

150g/5 oz plain chocolate,
    broken
25g/1 oz unsalted butter,
    diced
3 eggs
15ml spoon/1 tablespoon
    cognac, whisky or an
    orange liqueur, optional

TO DECORATE

whipped or plain cream,
    grated plain chocolate or
    chopped nuts

Melt the chocolate with the butter in a bowl placed over a saucepan of hot water, stirring occasionally until smooth.

Meanwhile, separate the eggs. Remove the bowl form the heat and stir in the egg yolks and spirit or liqueur if using.

Whisk the egg whites until stiff but not dry, then lightly fold into the chocolate.

Spoon into 4 cold individual dishes or glasses. Leave in a cool place for at least 15 minutes. Serve decorated with cream and chocolate or nuts, if liked.

LEMON SOUFFLÉS

 10 minutes + 15 minutes cooking

350g/12 oz Ricotta cheese,
    sieved
40g/1½ oz sugar
finely grated rind of 3 lemons
juice of 1½ lemons
3 egg whites, whisked

Beat the cheese with the sugar, then add the lemon rind and juice.

Fold in the egg whites and divide between 4 individual ovenproof dishes that have been buttered and lightly sprinkled with caster sugar.

Cook in a moderate oven, 180°C/350°F/Gas 4, for about 15 minutes until well risen.

WINE-POACHED RHUBARB

 10 minutes + 20–30 minutes cooking

450g/1 lb young rhubarb,
    trimmed and cut into
    4cm/1½ inch lengths
approx 50g/2 oz sugar
100ml/4 fl oz fruity dry white
    wine, eg Alsatian riesling
3 × 15ml spoons/
    3 tablespoons rosehip syrup

TO SERVE

chilled thick Greek yoghurt,
    perhaps flavoured with a
    little orangeflower water

Layer the rhubarb and sugar in a large ovenproof casserole. Pour the wine over, cover and cook for 20–30 minutes in a low oven, 170°C/325°F/Gas 3, until the rhubarb is tender but still retains its shape.

Carefully lift out the rhubarb with a perforated spoon. Pour the juices into a saucepan, stir in the rosehip syrup and boil until reduced and syrupy, then pour over the rhubarb.
Serve with yoghurt.

Note: Rosehip syrup adds depth to the flavour as well as sweetness. If it is not available, add a little extra sugar.

BASIC RECIPES

Fish stock
Chicken stock
Veal stock
Brown veal stock
Game stock
Filo pastry
Mayonnaise
Hollandaise sauce
Flavoured vinegars
Flavoured butters
Flavoured oils

FISH STOCK

20g/¾ oz unsalted butter
1 onion
white part of 1 leek, chopped
50g/2 oz mushrooms, chopped
1kg/2 lb 3 oz fish bones, heads
  and trimmings soaked in
  cold water for 3 hours
150ml/¼ pint medium-bodied
  dry white wine
bouquet garni of 1 bayleaf, 3
  parsley stalks and 1 sprig of
  fennel

Heat the butter, add the vegetables, cover and cook over a moderate heat, shaking the pan occasionally, for 4–5 minutes. Stir in the fish bones and trimmings and cook, stirring, for 2–3 minutes. Stir in the wine and reduce by half. Add the bouquet garni and about 1.75 litres/ 3 pints water, bring to the boil, remove the scum from the surface, then simmer for about 25 minutes, removing the scum from the surface occasionally.

Pass through a sieve lined with muslin or cheesecloth. Leave to cool, then remove all the fat from the surface.

CHICKEN STOCK

1kg/2 lb 3 oz chicken
  carcasses, necks, wings,
  feet, giblets except the liver
  or 1 boiling fowl, chopped
1 pigs trotter or veal knuckle
  bone, chopped
1 whole onion, spiked with 2
  cloves
1 carrot, sliced
1 stick of celery, sliced
white part of 2 leeks, sliced
bouquet garni of 1 bayleaf, 4
  parsley stalks, 1 sprig of
  thyme, 2 sprigs chervil

Put the chicken carcasses, bones and giblets, or the boiling fowl, and the pigs trotter or veal bone into a large saucepan. Cover with cold water and bring to the boil.

Carefully skim the scum from the surface, add the vegetables, bouquet garni and about 2 litres/3½ pints water. Return to the boil, remove the scum from the surface, then simmer for about 3 hours, removing the scum from the surface frequently.

Pass through a sieve lined with muslin or cheesecloth. Leave to cool, then remove all the fat from the surface.

VEAL STOCK

1kg/2 lb 3 oz veal knuckle
  bones, chopped
1 onion, studded with 1 clove
1 carrot, chopped
white part of 1 leek, chopped
1 stick of celery, chopped
bouquet garni of 1 bay leaf, 3
  parsley stalks, 1 sprig of
  thyme and 1 sprig of chervil

Blanch the bones in boiling water for 1 minute. Drain, then place in a large saucepan and cover with about 2 litres/3½ pints water. Bring to the boil, remove the scum from the surface, add the vegetables and bouquet garni and simmer for 3–4 hours or until the liquid is reduced to about 1 litre/1¾ pints.

Pass through a sieve lined with muslin or cheesecloth, leave to cool, then remove all the fat from the surface.

BROWN VEAL STOCK

*1kg/2 lb 3 oz veal knuckle
    bones and trimmings,
    chopped*
15ml spoon/1 tablespoon oil
1 onion, sliced
1 carrot, sliced
white part of 1 leek, sliced
1 stick of celery, sliced
*100g/4 oz mushroom
    trimmings*
*150ml/5 fl oz full-bodied dry
    white wine*
450g/1 lb tomatoes, chopped
*bouquet garni of 1 bayleaf, 1
    sprig of thyme, 4 parsley
    stalks and 1 sprig of
    tarragon*

Put the bones and trimmings into a roasting tin, pour the oil over and turn the bones so they are lightly coated in oil. Put into a hot oven, 220°C/425°F/Gas 7 until browned, turning frequently.

Stir the onion, carrot, leek and celery into the bones and return to the oven for about 10 minutes until browned. Stir in the mushroom trimmings, then tip the contents of the roasting tin into a large saucepan over a moderate heat.

Stir the wine into the roasting tin to dislodge the sediment and boil until reduced by half. Pour into the saucepan.

Add the tomatoes, bouquet garni and about 2 litres/$3\frac{1}{2}$ pints water. Bring to the boil, remove the scum from the surface and simmer gently for 3–4 hours, removing the scum from the surface frequently until the liquid is reduced to about 1 litre/$1\frac{3}{4}$ pints.

Pass the stock through a sieve lined with muslin or cheesecloth. Leave to cool, then carefully remove all the fat from the surface.

GAME STOCK

*1kg/2 lb 3 oz game carcasses,
    bones and trimmings,
    chopped*
15ml spoon/1 tablespoon oil
1 onion, studded with 2 cloves
1 carrot, chopped
1 stick of celery, chopped
white part of 1 leek, chopped
425ml/$\frac{3}{4}$ pint red wine
1 litre/2 pints veal stock
6 juniper berrries, crushed
6 coriander seeds, crushed
*bouquet garni of 1 bayleaf,
    4 parsley stalks, 1 sprig of
    sage and 1 sprig of thyme*

Put the game carcasses, bones and trimmings in a roasting tin, pour the oil over and turn the bones to coat them lightly in oil. Place in a hot oven, 220°C/425°F/Gas 7, or under the grill until lightly browned.

Add the vegetables and turn them to coat. Return to the oven or grill until lightly browned.

Tip the contents of the roasting tin into a large saucepan. Over a moderate heat, stir the wine into the roasting tin to dislodge the sediment, then boil until reduced by one third. Pour into the saucepan, stir in the stock and about 2 litres/$3\frac{1}{2}$ pints water. Add the juniper, coriander and bouquet garni. Bring to the boil, remove the scum from the surface, then simmer for 3–4 hours until the liquid is reduced to 1 litre/$1\frac{3}{4}$ pints, removing the scum from the surface frequently.

Pass through a sieve lined with muslin or cheesecloth. Leave to cool then remove all the fat from the surface.

FILO PASTRY

100g/4 oz strong plain flour
large pinch of salt
1 egg yolk, beaten
2 × 15ml spoons/
* 2 tablespoons melted*
* unsalted butter*
5ml spoon/1 teaspoon lemon
* juice*
approx 3–4 × 15ml
* spoons/3–4 tablespoons*
* warm water*
extra melted butter

Sieve the flour and salt onto a work surface and form a well in the centre.

Blend the egg yolk, butter and lemon juice together and pour into the well. Gradually draw the flour into the egg yolk mixture to form a soft, very pliable but not sticky dough, adding a little water, as necessary.

Form the dough into a ball and knead it well. Roll the dough into a long sausage shape then pick it up by one end and bang the other down on the work surface. Repeat the banging for several minutes, changing ends occasionally, until small bubbles appear on the surface of the dough and it is smooth, silky and very elastic. Alternatively, use a food processor for this stage.

Form the dough into a ball again and leave it to relax for 30 minutes under an inverted bowl.

Cover a large surface with a clean cloth and secure it underneath, if possible, then sieve a thin even layer of flour over the cloth.

Form the dough into a rectangle on the cloth, brush a little warm butter over it then roll it out as thinly as possible, taking care not to tear the surface. Brush the surface lightly again with a little more butter and leave the dough to relax for 3–4 minutes.

Lightly oil the backs of your hands. Put your hands under the dough, palms down, thumbs together, then gently push your hands apart to stretch the dough. Repeat, moving from one area to another, to ensure the dough is stretched to an even thickness.

Lightly brush any patches that begin to dry out with a little melted butter to soften them and keep the dough pliable. Continue stretching the dough for 15–20 minutes until it is almost transparent.

Cut away the thick border of dough that forms around the edge with a large pair of scissors. Cut the dough into large squares or rectangles and immediately cover with a damp cloth to prevent it drying out.

Use immediately, if required. Stack the rest interleaved with sheets of clingfilm. Roll the stack up and wrap with freezer-proof polythene. Filo pastry will keep, frozen, for 2–5 months.

To use the filo, remove the number of sheets required, keep them covered with a damp cloth and use as soon as they begin to soften. Wrap the roll again and return it to the freezer.

MAYONNAISE

Makes about 300ml/½ pint

1 egg yolk, at room temperature
5ml spoon/1 teaspoon mustard
300ml/½ pint olive oil or a blend of olive and a nut oil, at room temperature
2–3 × 5ml spoons/2–3 teaspoons white wine or herb vinegar or lemon juice, depending on taste and use
salt, freshly ground white pepper

Blend the egg yolks, or a whole egg if liked, with the mustard.

Beat in, drop by drop, 2 × 15ml spoons/2 tablespoons oil, beating well after each addition, then gradually beat in the remaining oil, increasing the amount of each addition as the sauce thickens, and beating well after each addition.

If the sauce separates or curdles, try beating in 15ml/1 tablespoon very hot water, or gradually beating the curdled sauce into another egg yolk, which must also be at room temperature.

Add vinegar or lemon juice and salt and pepper to taste.

Cover the surface closely with clingfilm and store the mayonnaise in a cool place. If this has to be the refrigerator, keep the mayonnaise in the warmest place, ie as far away from the chilling unit as possible. perhaps in the salad drawer or on the door. Keep for no longer than 2–3 days, or at most a week.

BLENDER OR FOOD PROCESSOR MAYONNAISE

This combines the dual advantages of saving time and being almost infallible. The results may not be quite as good as the best conventionally-made mayonnaise, but for most people on most occasions the advantages far outstrip any minor imperfections. Besides, if additional ingredients are added to the mayonnaise to flavour it and increase the originality of a dish, any slight changes in the flavour or texture can become undetectable to all but the most experienced of mayonnaise eaters.

If a whole egg is used, rather than 2 yolks, the sauce will be lighter and less rich, which some people prefer.

2 egg yolks, or 1 whole egg, at room temperature
2.5ml spoon/½ teaspoon Dijon mustard
300ml/½ pint olive or nut oil, at room temperature
2–3 × 5ml spoons/ 2–3 teaspoons wine or herb vinegar or lemon juice
salt, freshly ground pepper

Briefly blend the egg yolks or whole egg with the mustard, then, with the motor running, gradually pour in the oil, adding it very slowly at first but increasing the size of the additions as the sauce thickens. Add about a third of the vinegar or lemon juice after about half of the oil has been incorporated. Add the remaining vinegar or lemon juice and salt and pepper to taste.

FLAVOURINGS

Make 300ml/½ pint mayonnaise, using a flavoured oil or vinegar.

Tarragon: Use tarragon vinegar and add 2 × 15ml spoons/2 tablespoons chopped tarragon. Good with chicken, fish and eggs.

Mustard: Add an extra 2 × 15ml/2 tablespoons Dijon mustard. Good with steak tartare, smoked venison, all types of sausages, boudins etc.

Apple: Add 150ml/¼ pint thick apple purée to the finished sauce.

Watercress:	Add the leaves and fine stems from 1 bunch (about 100g/4 oz) watercress plus 5ml spoon/1 teaspoon lemon juice, just before serving. Use black pepper. Good with fish, chicken.
Horseradish:	Add 15ml spoon/1 tablespoon creamed horseradish to the finished sauce. Good with beef, salmon and cauliflower.

HOLLANDAISE SAUCE

Makes about 300ml/$\frac{1}{2}$ pint

15ml spoon/1 tablespoon
  lemon juice or white wine
  vinegar
5ml spoon/1 teaspoon crushed
  black peppercorns
1 blade of mace
2 egg yolks, beaten
175g/6 oz unsalted butter,
  melted
salt
lemon juice

Boil the lemon juice or vinegar, peppercorns and mace with 2 × 15ml spoons/2 tablespoons water in a small saucepan until reduced to 15ml spoon/1 tablespoon.

Remove from the heat. Remove the peppercorns and mace, then beat in the egg yolks.

Place the saucepan in a saucepan of hot water and beat with a wire whisk, making sure to reach into the corners of the saucepan, until the mixture becomes very creamy. Make sure the temperature of the eggs does not exceed 60°C/140°F. Gradually add the butter, whisking constantly, and whisking well after each addition. As the sauce begins to thicken, the butter can be added a little more quickly.

Season with salt and lemon juice.

Should the sauce curdle, add an ice cube and whisk furiously, over the water, until it becomes smooth again. Remove the ice cube immediately.

Note: Hollandaise sauce can be prepared up to 30 minutes in advance and kept warm over, not in, warm water. Whisk it frequently, to make sure that it does not separate. It can also be kept for up to two days in the refrigerator and reheated when required by whisking vigorously in a bowl placed over hot water, but there is a danger of the sauce separating.

BLENDER HOLLANDAISE

As with mayonnaise, the use of an electric blender can bring hollandaise within the repertoire of the person who is preparing high quality meals quickly. It also simplifies the preparation of a variety of hollandaise-based sauces that will enliven plainly cooked fish, meats, vegetables, eggs and pasta.

175g/6 oz unsalted butter,
  diced
15ml spoon/1 tablespoon
  lemon juice or white wine
  vinegar
3 egg yolks
salt, freshly ground white
  pepper
caster sugar, optional

In separate saucepans heat the butter until it has just melted, and the lemon juice or vinegar until bubbling.

Blend the egg yolks briefly in a blender then, with the motor running, slowly trickle in the lemon juice or vinegar. When the mixture is well blended, keep the motor running, and very slowly pour in the butter to give a smooth thick 'creamy' sauce. Season with salt and pepper and adjust the sharpness, if necessary, with lemon juice or caster sugar.

Maltaise sauce:	Use the juice of a blood orange instead of lemon juice for the final seasoning and add the finely grated rind. Good with firm white fish, trout, salmon, asparagus, celeriac or Jerusalem artichokes.
Seville orange hollandaise:	Use the rind and juice of a Seville orange instead of a blood orange. Good with pheasant.
Mousseline sauce:	Fold in 100ml/4 fl oz whipped cream just before serving and increase the seasoning.
Watercress hollandaise:	Add the leaves from a bunch (about 100g/4 oz) watercress, puréed with 15ml spoon/1 tablespoon white wine. Good with chicken, fish, shellfish and pasta.
Mint hollandaise:	Add 2 × 15ml spoons/2 tablespoons finely chopped mint. Good with lamb, pork, salmon, monkfish, duck, new potatoes, peas and mangetout peas.
Apple hollandaise:	Add 2 × 15ml spoons/2 tablespoons thick apple purée, lightly laced with Calvados, just before serving. Good with pork, duck, trout.
Horseradish hollandaise:	Add $1\frac{1}{2}$ × 5ml spoons/$1\frac{1}{2}$ teaspoons finely grated horseradish. Good with beef, trout, smoked trout and smoked salmon, if the horseradish flavour is kept light; cauliflower and pasta.
Mustard hollandaise:	Add 1–2 × 5ml spoons/1–2 teaspoons Dijon mustard. Good with eggs, fish, beef, lamb and parsnips.

FLAVOURED VINEGARS

HERB VINEGARS

300ml/½ pint volume of fresh herb leaves: basil, rosemary, lovage, thyme, marjoram, parsley, sage, mint, dill, fennel
600ml/1 pint white wine vinegar
sprigs of herb

Place the leaves in a wide-necked jar that they half fill, warm the vinegar and pour it over the herbs.

Cover the jar with an acid-resistant top and leave in a cool place for 4 weeks, shaking the jar daily. Leave the jar in a warm place, such as in front of a sunny window, to speed the process.

Taste the vinegar and if the flavour is well-pronounced, strain it through muslin into a clean bottle. Insert a sprig of fresh herb, stalk end first, into the bottle and close with an acid-resistant top.

If the vinegar does not taste strong enough, leave for another 1–2 weeks before bottling.

HERB VINEGAR USING SEEDS

Use 2 × 15ml spoons/2 tablespoons dill or fennel seeds, or 3 × 15ml spoons/3 tablespoons crushed toasted coriander seeds instead of the herb leaves. Add a long strip of lemon rind or 2 garlic cloves to dill or fennel.

Use the same method.

GARLIC VINEGAR

4 cloves fresh garlic, crushed
600ml/1 pint white wine vinegar

Put the garlic into a warm jar. Bring the vinegar to the boil, pour over the garlic and leave to cool.

Cover with an acid-resistant top and leave in a cool place for a week.

Proceed as for herb vinegar.

HORSERADISH VINEGAR

Use 40g/1½ oz grated horseradish to 600ml/1 pint vinegar and proceed as for garlic vinegar.

FRUIT VINEGAR

450g/1 lb fruit: raspberries, blackberries or blackcurrants
600ml/1 pint white wine vinegar
extra fruit
sugar, optional

Lightly crush a third of the fruit, pour the vinegar over, cover with a cloth and leave in a cool place for 24 hours.

Strain the vinegar through muslin onto another third of the fruit. Leave for 24 hours. Strain again through muslin onto the remaining fruit.

About a quarter fill a bottle with fresh fruit and strain the vinegar over. Cover with an acid-resistant top and leave in a cool, dark place for a month.

Up to 225g/8 oz sugar can be added to make a sweeter vinegar. Stir it into the vinegar in a non-aluminium saucepan over a low heat, then bring to the boil and leave to cool completely before finally pouring into bottles for storage.

Fruit vinegars can also be flavoured with spices and herbs to make some very interesting, tasty dishes–plum and ginger (use about 14 medium-sized halved and stoned plums, 6 thin slices fresh ginger and the grated rind of 1 lemon to 600ml/1 pint vinegar), or gooseberry and elderflower (use 225g/8 oz gooseberries, the grated rind of 1 lemon and a sprig of elderflowers), or juniper (use 6 juniper berries).

LEFT TO RIGHT:
HERB VINEGAR WITH ROSEMARY, CHIVES
AND FLAT PARSLEY; RASPBERRY VINEGAR;
CAPER OIL; GREEN PEPPERCORN OIL;
HERB VINEGAR WITH BASIL AND APPLEMINT;
FLOWER VINEGAR WITH CARNATION AND
WHITE ROSE PETALS

FLOWER VINEGAR

1 cup chopped scented flower petals
600ml/1 pint white wine vinegar

Put the petals into a wide-necked glass or stoneware jar, pour the vinegar over and leave at room temperature for a week, shaking the jar occasionally.

Strain the vinegar into a wide-necked bottle and add a few fresh petals for the decorative effect.

FLAVOURED BUTTERS

Simply beat the chosen flavouring into softened unsalted butter, adding a little lemon juice, if necessary, to 'lift' the flavour.

Store the butter in a covered pot or jar, or wrapped in cling film or polythene in the refrigerator or a cool place. Use it in cooking or as an accompaniment to transform vegetables, fish, shellfish, eggs, meats and pasta. Use it too to spread on toast, brioche or bread, or in a stuffing, eg smoked salmon butter inside rolls of fillets of sole.

Make the following flavoured butters with 175g/6 oz unsalted butter.

Garlic:	3 cloves finely crushed garlic.
Horseradish:	15ml spoon/1 tablespoon horseradish cream.
Lemon:	2 × 15ml spoons/2 tablespoons lemon juice and 15ml/1 tablespoon rind.
Lime:	2 × 15ml spoons/2 tablespoons lime juice and 2 × 15ml spoons/2 tablespoons rind.
Orange:	$1\frac{1}{2}$ × 15ml spoons/$1\frac{1}{2}$ tablespoons each orange juice and rind.
Mustard:	2 × 15ml spoons/2 tablespoons mustard.
Nut:	50g/2 oz finely chopped nuts of any kind.
Herb:	Approx 3 × 15ml spoons/3 tablespoons finely chopped herbs and 15ml/1 tablespoon lemon juice.
Anchovy:	Approx 6–8 mashed anchovy fillets that have been soaked in a little milk, then drained, and a large squeeze of lemon juice.
Smoked salmon:	175g/6 oz pounded smoked salmon and a large squeeze of lemon juice.
Green peppercorn:	15ml spoon/1 tablespoon chopped green peppercorns.
Stilton:	175g/6 oz crumbled Stilton.

Taste the butter after adding the flavouring and adjust the balance, if necessary, with more butter, flavouring, lemon juice or seasoning.

FLAVOURED OILS

HERB OIL

sprigs of fresh herbs:
  rosemary, thyme, tarragon,
  marjoram, fennel, dill, sage,
  basil, lemon balm or *a*
  combination of herbs
mild olive oil or *flavourless*
  vegetable oil
extra sprigs of herbs

Lightly bruise enough herbs to half fill a wide-necked glass jar or bottle when loosely packed in. Fill up with oil and leave in a warm place, such as a sunny window sill for 2 weeks, lightly shaking the bottle or jar every day.

Strain the oil through muslin, pressing down well on the herbs. Taste the oil to test the strength of the flavour. If it is not strong enough, leave the herbs to steep in the oil for a few days longer.

If the strength is right, pour the oil into a clean bottle, insert a sprig of fresh herb, if liked, and seal the bottle securely.

Store in a cool place away from direct sunlight.

Garlic oil: Substitute approx 3 crushed garlic cloves for the herbs and test after 1 week.

Flower oil: Substitute chopped flower petals or scented leaves such as rose, sweet geranium, fuchsia, carnation, marigold or nasturtium, for the herbs, filling the jar or bottle only half full.

Caper oil: Use large, well-drained capers and only half-fill the jar or bottle. Leave in a cool place for 10–14 days.

Peppercorn oil: Use 3 × 15ml spoons/3 tablespoons lightly crushed green or black peppercorns to 600ml/1 pint olive oil. Leave for 7–10 days.

INDEX

Numbers in *italics* refer to photographs